THE
GOLD

MW00696262

PROSPERITY
A guide to your Pearl Sequence

3 of 4

GENE KEYS

This edition published in Great Britain and USA 2018
by Gene Keys Publishing Ltd
Lytchett House, 13 Freeland Park
Wareham Road, Lytchett Matravers, Poole BH16 6FA

Copyright © Richard Rudd 2012, 2017, 2018
Cover design by Colour & Thing

All rights reserved. No part of this book may be reproduced
or utlised in any form or by any means, electronic or mechanical,
without prior permission in writing from the publishers.

Richard Rudd

THE GENE KEYS GOLDEN PATH

Prosperity: A guide to your Pearl Sequence

ISBN 978-1-9996710-2-0

The Gene Keys are neither science nor pseudo-science. They are presented as
a poetic exploration into consciousness that uses the 64 Codons of DNA as a
mystical metaphor for the holographic code underpinning all life. These teachings
are a labyrinth, and when you enter them with an open heart and mind, you may
move through a deep transformation resulting in a more compassionate view of
yourself and others. This book is designed for your inspiration. Neither the author
nor the publisher claim to dispense any psychological or other professional advice
in these pages. You read it with the understanding that you are fully responsible
for your own choices, actions and results. We accept no responsibility for your
impending good fortune.

GENEKEYS.COM

CONTENTS

1. Introduction   1

2. The pathway of initiative   15

3. The sphere of vocation   27

4. The sphere of culture   47

5. The pathway of growth   71

6. The sphere of your brand   81

7. The pathway of service   101

8. The sphere of the pearl   113

9. The pathway of the quantum   129

ABOUT THE AUTHOR

Richard Rudd is an international teacher, writer and award-winning poet. His mystical journey began early in life when he experienced a life changing state of spiritual illumination over 3 days and nights in his twenties. This catalysed an extensive worldwide spiritual search. All his studies became synthesised in 2002 when he began to write and receive the Gene Keys – a vast synthesis exploring the miraculous possibilities inherent in human DNA. It took seven years to write the book as well as understand and embody its teachings. Today Richard continues to study and teach the profound lessons contained in the Gene Keys.

FOREWORD

Philanthropy is not the privilege of the wealthy, but a requirement of the healthy. This statement is the foundation of the Pearl teachings in this book. As the third and final Part of the Golden Path journey, the Pearl brings these teachings to their crowning glory. If you have come this far then you are ready for a breakthrough in your life. This breakthrough may also come as a surprise to you. You may have the idea that breakthroughs are dramatic, like peals of thunder rolling around the sky.

Your breakthrough through the Pearl may be different. This is a teaching about Simplicity. Once the heart is opening through your Venus Sequence, it lends your life a whole new perspective - to be of greater service to the world. The 3 'P's of the Golden Path are synthesised in the Pearl - Purpose, Partnership and Prosperity - they each depend on each other and feed each other. May your heart find this vision of Simplicity and may your mind become lucid and clear.

Our world needs a new kind of human and a new approach to business. The Pearl describes this new philanthropic human and lays out the possibilities of a new approach towards money. Like the first two books on the Golden Path, this one is also designed to go with the online program, which adds valuable layers and insights to your journey of exploration into your Hologenetic Profile.

I would like to offer you my congratulations on having the commitment to come this far and in completing the Golden Path. I hope you have found it to be helpful and inspirational. May prosperity ripple out into your life, bringing you unseen joys as well as being a deep comfort in challenging times.

Richard Rudd

1. INTRODUCTION

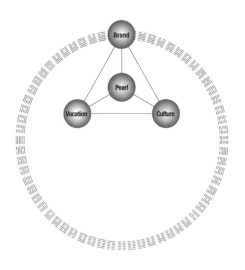

YOUR PEARL SEQUENCE
LIBERATING YOUR PROSPERITY

Welcome to Part 3 of the Golden Path - the Pearl. The Pearl brings the whole Golden Path to a glowing crescendo of consciousness. It is both a revelation and a conclusion. Your commitment to this path of contemplation shows that you have within you the capacity to embody these teachings at the deepest level. When we come to the Pearl, we will discover some final extraordinary twists in the tale of human consciousness. Here we will enter into the domain of the miraculous. We will invoke the possibilities of our common future - of a newly arising communal awareness that can bridge these seemingly separate biological vehicles, and forge a new kind of humanity whose higher purpose is to manifest the true meaning of prosperity.

The words that underpin the Gene Keys revelation are very carefully chosen. Every word resonates with a specific frequency. You will note that the title of the Pearl combines the two elements of Prosperity and Liberation - two words that are perhaps not often considered together. We will learn that the liberation of prosperity is about coming to a profound clarity of mind as well as gaining a vision of simplicity. We will also see how our capacity to thrive hinges on our ability to integrate both spiritual and material poles in our lives.

The other vital truth to be remembered here at the beginning of this third phase of your inner voyage concerns the relationship of your inner life to your outer life. In the introduction to the Golden Path, we may recall that the potential outcome of this journey is to attain a state known as *individuation*:

Individuation refers to a process whereby the many different aspects of your life - your dreams, your relationships, your health, your finances, your spirituality – are brought together into an integrated harmony.

An individuated human being is a person whose inner life is in exact harmony with their outer life. In such a person, everything has become simplified. The power of your aloneness is the font of your strength, but it in no way isolates you from your community. On the contrary, your aloneness serves to strengthen your bonds within your community. In an individuated being, many emotional states are naturally processed and transmuted internally, causing far less friction, confusion, or energy loss in the environment. This also brings far more ease and simplicity into all your relationships. The more individuated you become, the more energy efficient you become.

These words from the introduction remind us of the whole purpose of the Golden Path voyage - to purify, intensify, and clarify your inner life in order that it ripples out, and becomes manifest in your outer life. In the Activation Sequence, we learn to become anchored in a deep sense of purpose as a knowing within the cells of our physical body. This, in time, will lead to a life of higher purpose lived in the world. Similarly, the Venus Sequence teaches us gently to coax our hearts open by fully entering into the nature of our suffering and thereby transforming it. This, in time, will lead to the manifestation of many truly fulfilling and open-hearted relationships.

The Pearl Sequence naturally follows the Venus Sequence, as the harvest that arises from the first two sequences. Through the embodiment of our higher purpose and the opening of our heart, we engage the universe to assist us in our own higher destiny in the outer world. In the Pearl, we witness our true vocation choreographing the forces of synchronicity and bringing us into concert with a higher harmony involving many others operating at a similar frequency. In the Pearl, we also learn to further refine our outer expression through a continual contemplation of the essential in life.

CONTEMPLATING THE ESSENTIAL

What do we mean by contemplating the essential? This is the whole work of the Pearl. In our Pearl Sequence, we will contemplate 4 Spheres and their Gene Keys and lines. Through the Shadows of these Gene Keys, you will see the various ways in which your life *leaks* energy and vital power. The Pearl is like a mini-genetic circuit inside you - a *thrive capacitor* that condenses, fuses, and focuses the entire potential of your higher purpose into a single integrating zero point within you - the central Sphere known as *the Pearl*.

As you will see, half the secret of prosperity is knowing what prosperity really means for you. We may have an image of our life that is at odds with the natural flow of our destiny, and it is this conditioned image that actually blocks the flow of true prosperity from manifesting. As you continue to open your heart more within your relationships, your priorities and principles may well begin to change. What once seemed important to you, may well fade into the horizon of your past, to be replaced by a vision rooted in simpler qualities that you perhaps used to overlook. Contemplating the essential therefore has a lot to do with the architecture of your inner life - your secret desires and expectations, as well as your unconscious beliefs and dreams.

As we enter into the realm of our Pearl Sequence, we shift planes once again - this time from the emotional/astral plane to the mental plane. The Pearl teaches us about the true nature and power of thought. We will come to see thinking as an extension of our deepest essence. It is a whirling emanation that can stir hidden forces into action, and instead of trapping us into a tight inner world of limiting beliefs, it can open us up to a wholehearted experience of consciousness at play.

THE MONEY QUESTION

Our modern world, whether we like it or not, revolves around money. We have become so used to this, that very few of us question it or even contemplate what the world might be like without money. As adults, money occupies a huge part of our thoughts and feelings. It is an intriguing truth, that it is very hard to find a person in the world who doesn't wish he or she had more money! The Pearl opens up this subject of money for deep contemplation. Much has already been spoken on the subject of money, and much money has been made by people speaking on the subject! As the goal of the Venus Sequence is to open our hearts, the goal of the Pearl is to help us to fully prosper. And just as we open our hearts by forgiving ourselves and by taking a softer approach, so we learn to prosper by dropping our mental tightness around money. In both cases, we are learning to open inwardly rather than doing anything externally.

The Pearl gives us a new vision of the world. It even goes so far as to envisage a world where money is no longer needed. In this sense, it is a teaching ahead of its time, but it also provides us with a bridge to this extraordinary future. Sometimes we need to step fully beyond our current set of mental parameters, in order to see the present moment with clarity. A great deal of the wisdom of the Pearl involves seeing with clarity. Once we can see our own mind with absolute clarity, then the habits we have learned, and the anxiety we feel about money can dissipate. Remarkably, for most people, prosperity comes simply through deep mental clarity.

As we gain a new inner clarity through the Pearl, so we may well begin to make adjustments to our lives externally. This need not be through any conscious technique or strategy, but can emerge organically and in its own time. In the Golden Path, the Pearl is like the coda in a piece of music. It takes the momentum of the first two sequences and brings them to a structural conclusion. It also draws together all the elements of the whole Golden Path, and threads them into a complete tapestry.

Prosperity is therefore a result of purpose, and it follows and flows through an open-hearted approach to life. It also allows you the traveller to distil the contemplative wisdom that you have garnered along the way, and bring it to bear on your own life in a practical way. In this regard the Pearl is an exciting moment in your evolution, because it offers you the inner proof of the validity of your engagement, and is the reward of your commitment.

THE PURPOSE OF LIFE IS TO THRIVE

When we began our journey along the Golden Path, we began by contemplating our higher purpose. The Activation Sequence teaches us that purpose is not only an external journey, but a deep-seated knowing in our DNA. To touch into your own higher purpose is to come fully into the present moment, into the wonderful vibrant pulse of life inside our body. When we feel and know our purpose as our essence, then we radiate health and vitality. Our body thrives and this thriving is life itself breathing through us. In the Venus Sequence, hologenetically folded up like a series of Russian dolls inside the Sphere of our Purpose, we learn what it means to thrive in relationship. Our hearts open in love and friendship, and we discover the higher purpose hidden in the chemistry of each relationship in our lives.

This gradual opening and softening also gives us a greater core stability, lending us a new strength from the inside out. In the Pearl, this opening extends further into our community through our work. Whatever our work is -

whether it is a role in the business community, a creative impulse, or a role in service, that work is a potential outlet for our ability to thrive within the greater community of humanity. Purpose therefore has a threefold nature as it knits together our physical health, our ability to love and be loved, and our working life. When we are prospering, then all three of these aspects of our life are in harmony. The mystery of the Golden Path is that it shows you the natural sequence that brings this harmony about.

Our sense of purpose is vital for our physical body to thrive. Without our basic self-esteem that comes from our 4 Prime Gifts, we cannot progress any further along the Golden Path. The Venus Sequence will remain locked to us. However, as soon as we activate this deep feeling of inner purpose, then we have a strong foundation for entering the profound voyage of our Venus Sequence. And as we begin to open our hearts to life once again through the teachings of our Venus Sequence, then we will begin to experience the spontaneous flowering of the Pearl as the forces of good fortune and prosperity flow into our life.

PROSPERITY V WEALTH

Before we enter into a contemplation of our Pearl Sequence, we need to have a clear understanding of the difference between prosperity and wealth. Wealth can be seen as the stockpiling of energy or money. It is generally regarded as a healthy thing to have as much money as possible in order to feel secure in life. This widely held belief drives much of our society. The Pearl however directly challenges the urge or need to create wealth. Wealth is heavy. Rather than creating freedom and a sense of purpose, it tends to create a deep energetic drag in our lives. The more we have, the more we feel a need to spend it. And the more we spend it, the more complicated our lives become. We accumulate more *stuff* and more responsibilities. We humans so often complicate our lives without even realising it.

This natural tendency to want to spend the money we have (and indeed the money we don't have!) is worthy of further consideration. Why do we feel the need to do this? Perhaps the reason lies deeper than we realise. When we look at nature, we see a similar pattern. Once the fruit has flowered, the tree drops it to the ground. Nature doesn't hoard. Nature is constantly flowering and releasing in tune with the seasons. This is the great secret of prosperity - the secret of flow. Whereas wealth stagnates, prosperity is a flow. We receive and then we give, creating a vacuum into which life once again flows.

Prosperity is also about more than spending the energy we have accumulated - it is about spending it in the right way. It is about spending it on the essential - on that which enhances, inspires, simplifies, and lightens, rather than on the inessential, which drains, burdens, and complicates your life.

As you enter into the transmission of the Pearl, you are invited to begin an inventory of your own life. You may wish to look around your home and consider the things which are essential, as opposed to those which are inessential. William Morris, the father of the Arts and Crafts Movement in the nineteenth century famously said: "Have nothing in your house that you do not know to be useful, or believe to be beautiful".

You can also extend this inventory of the essential to other areas - the most important of all being your time. How do you spend your time? What does the *essential* mean for you? For most people, essential time refers to two things: time to fulfill our basic responsibilities and time for personal enrichment. What does personal enrichment mean to you and what importance do you place on it? To experience the flow of prosperity in your life, you will need to know the answers to these questions.

Prosperity is a state of mind. It is an attitude, a knack, and a delight we must learn to cultivate. The Pearl will repeatedly ask you to look at the ways in which you accumulate weight: this can be physical, emotional, and intellectual. There is no judgement in any of this - we are simply having the courage to look honestly at ourselves once again. Through the Venus Sequence, you have already shown this courage and inner honesty. Now we will extend this honesty to our material lives, and our mental beliefs and attitudes.

TO PROSPER IS TO SERVE

The above statement, simple though it sounds, unlocks another of life's great secrets - that through giving our time in service to a higher purpose, we can find a short-cut to prosperity.

This is the mystical version of a *get rich quick* program! When our heart opens fully in the Venus Sequence, it naturally floods us with the urge to share our love as widely as possible. Unconditional love is a kind of healthy pressure inside us, like a lustrous raincloud looking for a dry pasture to fall upon. Most of the world's great mystical traditions and religions have this urge to do good at their heart. The trick is to *do good* for the right reason, and in the right way, at the right time. Your Pearl Sequence will help you to see how and where you are best *designed* to serve your higher purpose.

The urge to be of service, although highly noble, can also be a great inner trap. It is one of the many ways in which the Shadow frequency can distract us away from our own deeper issues. Sometimes we give, in order not to have to receive. For many of us, receiving love is the thing we secretly yearn for the most, and it is also the thing we fear the most. To prosper, our lives must be an equal balance of giving and receiving. We must serve ourselves, our relationships, and the world in equal measure. You can look again at your own life, and see whether any of these areas are *overweight* or *underweight*. The Pearl will help you to redress this balance. We may be wealthy on the material plane, but unlucky in love, or we may have a loving relationship, but struggle with money. Prosperity cannot be compartmentalised, but is a *total* phenomenon, embracing all aspects of our lives simultaneously. It is unifying, simple, and surprisingly easy to bring into your life.

THE MONEY TRIANGLE - THE STRUCTURE OF THE PEARL

Your Pearl Sequence operates in a different way from the other two Sequences that comprise the Golden Path. Although it still unlocks in a sequence, it creates an energetic vortex in your life. At the centre of this vortex is the Pearl itself - the crystalisation of your prosperity. Your Pearl blooms as a reward unlocked by the currents of Grace. It is the result of a quantum effect that is triggered through the manifestation of your higher purpose on the material plane.

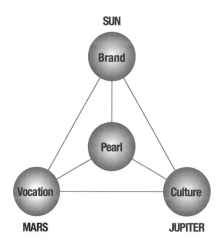

11

The mystery of the Golden Path occurs as we embody its truths. Your Hologenetic Profile offers a limited two-dimensional view of these truths. It is simply a pathworking tool that we can use to remind us of the various universal principles that bring about prosperity on all levels. The Pearl Sequence is structured as a triangle with a central hub. Each point of this triangle is imprinted through one of three planetary archetypes. These are Mars, Jupiter, and the Sun - three of the great masculine archetypes in the heavens. Just as the Venus Sequence is a feminine transmission, so the Pearl is more masculine.

The world of money has always seemed to require a more masculine approach - at least that is, until now. Following the Venus Sequence, the Pearl describes a completely new approach to money that is so radical, it will likely take many centuries to be fully realised.

The basis of the Pearl is the universal principle of Philanthropy. Philanthropy is the intelligent and healthy redistribution of energy within a system that brings a higher harmony to that system, allowing it to fully thrive and transcend its own limitations. This redistribution is not only material, but also mental and emotional.

As we have seen in the Venus Sequence, intelligence requires that our ideas and impulses come into alignment with higher principles, so it is often our thoughts and beliefs that have to change first of all. This is the other reason why the Pearl has a more masculine orientation - because it is about the mind as opposed to the emotions. Your Pearl Sequence reorients your thinking around money, and the whole concept of *making money*. We do not make money. We watch money come in, and we watch it go out. The trick then is not about *making* money. As we shall see, the trick is all in the watching.

THE EYE OF HORUS - THE EYE OF THE NEEDLE

For millenia mankind has used symbols to encode the truths we have discovered. The power of a symbol is that it lends itself to being understood across many dimensions. We can understand it mentally, we can see it visually, and we can sense its meaning intuitively. One of the symbols used by many cultures is that of the all-seeing eye. In Egyptology this is known as the *eye of Horus*. The eye of Horus also appears as the eye of providence, and famously appears on the back of the US one dollar bill. The eye is a symbol of the unbroken awareness of the siddhic state of consciousness. It might therefore seem unusual to see it connected to money and to providence or fortune.

The all-seeing eye represents the eternal present moment, and our ability to rest in this moment is the secret to unlocking true prosperity. To live in the present moment is to live with lightness, without baggage, or worries. Prosperity demands that we drop our mental projections of the world, and our dreams of how our life might be better one day.

Prosperity has nothing to do with money or with the future - it is the living current of vital presence that is ever-emerging from our Core. Money is one of the great sticking places for our addictive thinking. We think we need more money, but that train of thinking constantly pulls us out of the present moment where prosperity lives.

The Pearl teachings, like all the Gene Keys teachings, are founded upon universal truths. When Christ spoke the words: *It is easier for a camel to go through the eye of a needle than for a rich man to enter the kingdom of God* - he spoke a great truth. He was talking about the difference between wealth and prosperity. To prosper is to be light in consciousness, rather than being weighed down by our perception. The mistake we make is to try and find happiness. We tend to believe that happiness has to do with having more money, so we trap ourselves in a net of our own expectations and hopes.

The very word *prosper* is rooted in the Latin meaning to hope for. We hope for happiness in the future, instead of accepting that which is in the present. And in the present, we find something far greater than happiness - we find fulfilment. To be fulfilled means to be at ease deep inside your own being. Happiness comes and happiness goes. Sadness comes and sadness goes. But fulfilment is the field that lives behind both poles, and fulfilment is analogous to true prosperity.

2. THE PATHWAY OF INITIATIVE

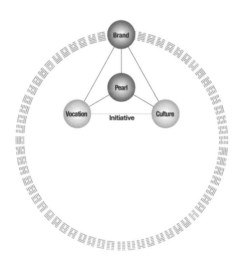

Welcome to the final part of your threefold voyage of contemplation! We begin with a contemplation of the Pathway of Initiative. Before we dive once again into the personalised aspect of your Profile - the Spheres - we will consider the motivating force that drives all prosperity - initiative. When I first began my own deep exploration of the meaning of prosperity, I found myself asking the fundamental question: *what is the core foundation of prosperity?* Over the following days as I cleared away thought pattern after thought pattern, I finally came to my revelation. The answer I received was that prosperity is about the ability to make fire.

This answer to me was wonderful and explosive. As a lover of myth, I immediately thought of the great legend of Prometheus, who famously stole fire from the gods. And in the same vein I thought about the legend of Icarus, whose lust for freedom drove him to fashion a pair of wings and then fly too close to the sun, whereupon the wax holding together the feathers melted, and he plummeted to his doom. What then does it mean to make fire? In these legends both protagonists are punished for their initiative, which to me simply shows that all initiative involves risk and fear.

If you mentally strip yourself down to your basic humanity without any of your external trappings and you put yourself in a pure survival situation, what is the most essential skill that gives you the confidence to survive? One answer might be the ability to make fire with your bare hands from the raw materials in your environment. In a survival situation, the ability to make fire does more than keep you warm and allow you to cook food or signal for help. In a survival situation, where fear can so easily dominate, everything changes from the moment you make a fire. The ability to make fire actually ignites your intelligence. It reinforces self-assurance and the healthy mental attitude that maximises your potential to survive. Although not as essential as water or air to life, fire is the one element we have to create ourselves, from our own deep inner resources. This is what makes fire such a good symbol for prosperity.

DARE TO BE DIVINE

As you get to this stage along your Golden Path, it is time for a wake-up call. We have spent a considerable time contemplating our Shadows, our Gifts, and our Siddhis. Now it is time to open our eyes and remove all our mental notions of progression and spiritual evolution. You may have discovered by now that the Gene Keys teachings are a web of contradictions and paradoxes, in particular when it comes to the Siddhis. The fact is that there is no specific goal behind the Gene Keys teachings. If you have a goal in mind, like the raising of the frequency of your awareness, then the Pearl is the part of this wisdom that will help you to let go of your spiritual goals in order that you can settle yourself more deeply into the present.

We humans are not wholly comfortable with paradoxes. And yet paradox is the only way to come close to Truth. Your journey along the Golden Path is a mystery, and it will not yield up its truths to a tight, questing mind. This is why we began the whole journey with a contemplation of the power of pause. It is only in the pauses, when time stands still, that you can become aware of Truth. One of the greatest gifts that comes from treading the Golden Path is a rising of creative initiative in your life. We each have to steal fire from the gods, in our own unique never-to-be-repeated way.

Because of the limitations of our thinking, it would not have been possible to write the Gene Keys book without laying it out through the spectrum of consciousness with its levels of frequency - the Shadow, the Gift, and the Siddhi. This structure is very helpful to us as we begin our contemplative journey. It is also very useful to us at an emotional level as we navigate the Venus Sequence. Our hearts relax when they are allowed to open in layers, rather than feeling pressured to open all at once. The final joke of the Golden Path comes in Part 3 as we navigate the mental realm. The threefold structure must be smashed altogether, as we clarify our thinking through the Pearl Sequence.

As we move through the Pearl and look once again at the Gene Keys, we must look with a beginner's mind. We must come to realise that the Shadow, the Gift, and the Siddhi are a single unified field. The lesson of Icarus is clear - freedom is a wild goose chase. The higher we go, the further we will fall. But Prometheus teaches us another lesson entirely - to be cheeky enough to steal those Siddhis from the gods. We must come to realise that the Siddhis are not faraway goals, but ordinary states that flicker in and out of our consciousness all the time without our permission. The Shadows too emerge out of the fire, and they can be every bit as beautiful as the rubescent flames that meet us as we gaze into the fire of the Siddhis. This then is your challenge - to take the initiative and dare to be divine - not as a perfect kind of superhuman beyond all suffering, but as a fallible, mortal, ordinary, but fiercely courageous human, down to earth and rooted in the earth.

TIME AND MONEY

There is a fascinating connection between money and time. The well worn cliche *time is money* hints at another fundamental truth concerning prosperity. There is a grand collective illusion that having money means that we will have more time. If you pause to contemplate this for a while, you may well find yourself laughing. Although money can buy you more *leisure time*, it doesn't alter time itself. Only perception alters time. If you are already unhappy inside yourself, then whether you are working or not working, you are never truly at ease. The dream of wealth is thus a flawed dream. Human beings spend lifetimes chasing this dream, and it can never, ever bring you peace or fulfilment.

Knowing the above, you can save yourself a great deal of pain and disappointment. The Pearl invites you to let go of the illusion that money will in any way help you to find fulfilment. At the same time we should not confuse fulfilment with comfort. A large proportion of the world population still lives in poverty.

If you are truly poor then in most cases, money will make your life much easier. And yet money can also make our lives more complicated. The complication comes in whenever we start wishing we had more. Prosperity is an invisible line in each person's life - it provides us with the exact amount of resources we need to fulfill our genius. For some people those resources are simple and fairly minimal, and for others they can be considerable. It all depends upon our Dharma, our higher life purpose.

Everything about prosperity is about balance. You have to balance peacefulness with practicality. If you live only for the moment without a care for the future, then your life will move out of balance. If you put all your energy into saving for the future, but miss out on the joyousness of life as it passes you by, then also you will be out of balance. Prosperity means that you can live both poles. It doesn't have very much to do with money at all. It has to do with your ability to see life with clarity.

PHYSICAL CONTEMPLATION - ARCHWAY INTO TIMELESSNESS

The beauty of life's pauses is that they enable us to see life with crystal clear vision. A day alive with pauses is a day rippling with awareness. As your contemplation of the Gene Keys continues to deepen, so your heart softens. As we soften, so we experience life through the all-seeing eye. The eye is that part of us that exists in the gaps and pauses. It sees life without thought, because it is the very space between our thoughts. Our inner eye opens as our contemplation moves from the mental dimension to the emotional, and from the emotional to the physical. In the pauses we stop what we are doing and for a brief moment we simply stare ahead. In these moments, which occur more regularly than most of us realise, we experience the unbroken field of consciousness that lives behind our life.

Physical Contemplation comes about as we sink into the depths of our life. The Golden Path gives us this step-by-step process by which we can lower ourselves into this most magical sense of spaciousness.

In many ways it tricks us into relaxing more deeply than we ever believed possible. As our emotional awareness penetrates behind the wounds that obscure the love and purity of our heart, so we plummet into our core. We move through life with what the Zen tradition aptly terms *choiceless awareness*. We watch ourselves making decisions, and then we watch the outcome of those decisions.

Every pause you become aware of is an archway of awareness leading to an experience of timelessness. At first, these can be simply fleeting moments that are soon interrupted by our thinking. However, as the process of physical contemplation continues to deepen, so your daily life becomes more punctuated by the silent backdrop of consciousness. Each pause is like a pinprick of light in the screen of our busyness. The more pauses that go on appearing, the more we become aware of the screen. And the nature of the pause is a beautiful thing. The pause brings us into the physical body, into the moment of our breathing, into our belly and our spine. The pause can also become quite blissful, so that we enjoy prolonging it. We may not do so consciously, but our body shows us how to luxuriate in the liquid field of the timeless. We learn the art of lingering.

FROM TRANSFORMATION TO CLARITY

On a practical level, a pause is anything that breaks the continuity of our activity. It could be a red traffic light when we are in a hurry, an unwelcome queue, or a talkative stranger. These are examples of pauses that we might resist. On the other hand, a pause can also be a rare bird crossing our path, an unexpected exchange of transparency with another person, or simply a deep in-breath as we realise how tired we feel. Pauses come in so many different forms, but the moment we become attuned to them, we discover their welcome presence everywhere.

As we slow down inwardly, we also come to another great point of revelation. At a certain juncture in our inward journey, we come to the end of transformation.

Transformation is a word of the heart, but not of the head. We experience transformation through the Venus Sequence, but through the Pearl we realise that that which is essential never changes. Our Core remains the same no matter what our life experiences bring us. This is the dawning of clarity, of mental acuity. Our mind begins to settle. Because our contemplation moves deeper into the physical body, the mind becomes clearer, sharper, and more insightful. By seeing the nature of our mind more clearly, we become less taken in by its vagaries.

This clarity of perception grows like a lens inside us, and as it does so, we begin to break out of our mental victim patterns. Our thinking offers us some of the most stubborn patterns to crack open. As with our emotional awareness, all it takes is seeing the pattern repeating in our lives, for the pattern to gradually lose its hold on us. One such pattern might be our struggle with money. Many people simply cannot see themselves as prosperous, because of the unconscious mental belief patterns they hold.

THE 'SPIRITUAL MISTAKE' WITH MONEY

The *Spiritual Mistake* refers to the tendency of those on a spiritual path to forget that they are human, and overlay their ordinary character traits with new ones that seem more *holy*. This tendency can also refer to our relationship to money, material success, and prosperity. Many seekers believe that spirituality comes about through adopting a particular lifestyle. This lifestyle is usually more meditative than materialistic, involves healthier eating patterns or specific diets, and usually some form of dedicated spiritual practise. There are elements of truth to all such things. For example, a disciplined spiritual practise may bring about a shift in our awareness. And as our awareness becomes more refined, we may well decide to eat and live more simply. However, clarity of awareness does not require any special set of external conditions nor can it necessarily be enhanced by them. If these things occur along the way, they may simply be a cultural by-product of our attempt to become awakened.

One of the hallmarks of prosperity is the ability to enjoy life. This means that we needn't live an austere existence, but are here to explore life in its many rich forms. Earning a healthy income is surely one of the ways in which we can enjoy and appreciate life. The spiritual mistake with money is not being able to earn enough to enjoy life. Many of us simply fall into a tendency to just about *get by*. Perhaps we do not believe that our lives can be any other way. If you are fully committed to the Golden Path, then you need to ask yourself a serious question: *can you truly see yourself as prosperous?* There is no discrepency between earning a healthy income and being awake. If you are not materially prosperous already, perhaps you have not quite answered this question truthfully inside yourself.

THE PATHWAY OF INITIATIVE - ACTING FROM GENIUS

When we first began this journey along the Golden Path we came into it via the Activation Sequence, whose subtitle is *Discovering your Genius.* Your genius refers to the activation of those creative components (the Gifts) within your Profile. Although it is seen at this early stage as consisting of your 4 Prime Gifts, your genius can be referred to all the Gene Keys and lines of your Profile. It is one thing to feel the essence of your genius emerging, but it is another to act it out in the world. This is what the Pearl Sequence is about, and it is why it begins with the Pathway of Initiative. Money comes through initiative.

Initiative comes from deep within you. It is your ability to make fire out of the tools in your environment. These tools of course are your Gifts. If you love something, then you will always have the enthusiasm and will to become good at it, which is why you should always do what you love in life. As you enter into your Pearl Sequence, you may feel an inner call to take action. The Pearl is contemplation in action. Action that is in harmony with life is action that arises out of the stillness and clarity of perception that we have already discussed. We are here to enjoy being, but we are also here to enjoy doing.

The Pearl is really all about acting. Life has often been likened to a theatre, where we are the actors or players. If we are here to act out a drama, then we might as well give it everything. We might as well choose a character we resonate with, rather than a dull echo of who we always wanted to be. It takes great courage to take the initiative in life. You will have to make some kind of inner and outer leap. It is interesting that the Gift of the 51st Gene Key is called the Gift of Initiative, and it is perhaps even more interesting that the 51st Siddhi is called the Siddhi of Awakening. A major part of what it means to be awake is about being willing to play the full role we are given at birth.

The Pearl challenges you to act from your genius and earn a healthy reward for doing so. This is not a difficult thing to do. To live according to your higher nature is the simplest thing in the world. For many of us however, following the initiative of our genius takes a great deal of courage. We will have to give up a world of compromise. We may have to take a calculated risk. One thing is for sure however - that when you take the leap and follow your genius out into the world, you will feel immediately better about yourself, your life and everything. At the deepest level, it will no longer matter as much to you whether you succeed or fail on a material level. The important thing is that you will have donned your costume, and acted out your role with conviction and pride.

THE PURPOSE OF WORK

As adults, a huge proportion of our time in life is given over to work. Considering this, it is perhaps strange how little thought we give to the purpose of work in our lives. We may assume that the purpose of work is to make money to support ourselves and those closest to us. This is of course true at a purely material level, but what about at other levels? From the point of view of the Golden Path, your work is an extension of your higher purpose, which is to open your heart. So once your heart is more open, then your natural impulse is to express your love through your work. Maintaining a healthy balance between work and relationships is one of the key factors underpinning a prosperous and fulfilling life. Perhaps the deepest underlying purpose of work is to relate, to create, and to inspire? We create and exchange resources with each other because we may need them, but the exchange itself is often the most potentially fulfilling part of the process. As you enter into your Pearl Sequence, you will see that prosperity cannot exist in isolation, but requires connection, teamwork, and mutually beneficial exchange.

Doing the right work also ensures our health. When we do what we love, then we feel the breath of inspiration moving within us. We have that most magical experience of being a vessel for the creative evolutionary impulse. We feel alive and excited by the challenges of each day, and the by-product is our physical health. This is the most essential definition of prosperity - to be alive. To be alive is to feel grateful for each experience and each day of our relatively short lives. It is this outpouring of gratitude that is the basis of health and prosperity. When we cave into life, when we forget why we are here, when we lose our sense of perspective, then we cease to feel grateful. There is always someone somewhere in a worse predicament than ours, and there is always someone handling the depths of their suffering with grace. Gratitude is perhaps the greatest of all human attributes - it is the oxygen of your soul.

You are alive, therefore you are already prospering.

3. THE SPHERE OF VOCATION

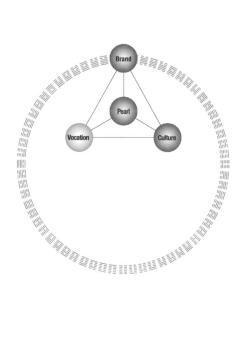

THE SPHERE OF YOUR VOCATION - ASKING THE RIGHT QUESTION

One of the greatest modern myths for the western world is that of the Quest for the Holy Grail. Although this myth has ancient, even neolithic roots, the myth of today has been shaped and adapted over the last thousand years by the changing western cultural psyche. For some mysterious reason it stands apart from all the more traditional redemptive myths. The Quest for the Grail is not a myth of redemption. It is a myth of reconciliation. What this means is that the hero, whose name is Perceval, does not go through the usual mythical transformation, where the spirit of grace intercedes to bring about wholeness. Perceval brings about his own healing, and in doing so, he challenges thousands of years of unconscious conditioning.

In the Venus Sequence, we complete our journey with the Sphere of your Core. This represents the place of the Core Wound in your psyche. Your journey through the underworld of the Shadows is a classic quest for redemption, in which your own open heart is progressively realised as your own inner saviour. The final journey of consciousness along the Pathway of Realisation is an expression of the reunion of our lower nature (the Shadow), with our higher nature (the Siddhi), culminating in the dawning of the enlightened consciousness. You might think that the story ends there. Most of the myths that we have ingested (whether as children or as adults) through metaphors, novels or films, do indeed end here at the point of inner wholeness. The values of modern humanity are based upon this self-serving, self-realised, self-driven perception.

The Pearl, however, represents the bud of a new world teaching that is only now coming into the world. In the near future, the world will need to harness the wisdom of this transmission if we are to surmount the next great global challenge that is coming. In the Grail myth, the Core Wound is symbolised by the figure of the wounded king (sometimes called the *fisher king*).

The King represents the old patriarchal model of the universe, which is why your Core Wound is calculated from the position of the planet Mars while you were still in the womb. Mars represents the immature aspect of the male psyche. Furthermore, the King's wound is extended in the legend to the land itself, which becomes the 'wasteland'. We have seen through the Venus and Saturn Sequences how the personal wound is genetically linked to the racial and planetary wound.

In the myth, the Grail itself represents the possibility of wholeness and healing, although it has been unable to fully heal the King's wound despite its power. The great turning point in the Grail myth comes when the young Perceval approaches the wounded King and asks a simple and very courageous question: *How can I serve the Grail?* This question is mythically encoded in the fabric of every human being. It sleeps in our very DNA. Instead of using the Grail to bring about his own wholeness, Perceval performs the greatest act of selflessness, wisdom, and generosity. The question is wise, because Perceval has realised that his own healing is intimately linked to the healing of the whole. And the reason that this myth is so relevant to our contemporary culture is because of one word - generosity. By offering to serve the whole, Perceval has transcended the need for Divine intervention. He has even sidestepped the need for transformation. He has realised that the opposing forces of nature can only be reconciled through asking the right question and then living the answer.

Your Pearl Sequence is an ongoing contemplation of the nature of this great inner question - how can I be of the greatest service to the whole? As you dive into the Pearl, you may well be surprised by the simplicity of the answer that comes.

YOUR VOCATION - THE GIFT IS IN THE GIFT

We begin our journey with the Sphere of your Core Wound, which now becomes the Sphere of your Vocation. Vocation is a lovely word that carries the notion of an inner calling. At a certain point in your inner journey, your Core Wound does indeed call you out into the world. There comes a time when you simply have to stop *processing*.

We will not attain the perfection our mind is looking for. There is nothing to attain. The magic comes when you open up enough of a highway into your heart, so that the Shadow state no longer dominates your life. Remember, we are not looking for complete redemption. We are here to bring about reconciliation of the opposing forces within us. Spiritual enlightenment is no longer on the menu! We can let go of those notions and the idea that the Shadow and Siddhi are so far apart. The gift is in the Gift!

The Gift frequency is where the Holy Grail lives. The Grail is not found as we might imagine in the Siddhi. The Gift frequency is where the human heart resides. It is where creativity and genius reside. The more we open our hearts to life and to others, the more we close the illusory gap between the Shadow and the Siddhi. Your Gifts are like wormholes that reconcile the opposites inside you; not through any attainment, but through a clear perception and embodiment of their creative potential. As your SQ opens, so it triggers the flowering of your vulnerability as your single-most creative calling - your Vocation. And through the Pearl, as you learn to don your actor's cloak and live out your Vocation, so in time it becomes your Life's Work, the outer expression of that core talent.

THE SHADOW

The Shadow of your Vocation is simply that you do not follow your vocation. In the Grail myth, Perceval has to overcome the rigid constraints of his upbringing before he can ask the right question. The Shadow has us believe that we will not prosper from doing the thing we most love. Our fear of taking the initiative keeps us locked inside ourselves. Worse still, it keeps us from transmuting our suffering into gold. This Sphere is the place where we are most wounded, and is therefore where we have the greatest capacity to prosper. But if we do not take the lunge, then all we have is our suffering without a sense of purpose to it. This is what brings about a life of struggle.

The Shadow of your Vocation can also be expressed as postponement. We postpone our higher purpose until we have enough money, until we have opened our heart enough, until our children have grown up. Whatever the excuse we find, it enables us to kid ourselves that we cannot, or are not, ready to take the initiative and unleash our creative, rebellious spirit. The simple fact is that we are afraid. It is very understandable that we should fear the unknown, and yet all of life is about the unknown. If we cling to the known, then we can never feel the surge of our vocation as it emerges into the world, bringing reconciliation both to the wound within and the world without.

THE GIFT

Your vocational Gift emerges as you live a more courageous life. You will never feel truly ready to meet the great challenge of your Vocation. Because it is rooted in your wound, it requires a great stretch of your entire being, but when you do take the initiative, suddenly you will find the fear diminishes to be replaced with excitement. You will draw the resources you need to meet the challenge of your higher Vocation from the wellspring of your core wound. You will find that you have an unbounded enthusiasm and indomitable spirit of perseverance in tackling any obstacles that you meet. These are all facets of the Gift of your Vocation.

The Sphere of your Vocation deserves perhaps the deepest contemplation of any of the Spheres along the Golden Path. It contains layers of meaning and magic that can radiate out into your life as you peel open its insights. It is here that you will discover your Core Talent - the mysterious quintessence gifted to you at conception by the hidden forces that choreograph human destiny. Look deeply into the Gift of your Vocation and its line. Let your whole life and contemplation revolve around the hub of this Gift. If you do not understand it, then remember to be patient.

Insight comes through perseverance, and it often comes at you from life through some kind of a reflection. To unlock the Gift of your Vocation is no small feat - it will always take courage, a certain level of risk, and a great deal of devotion.

THE SIDDHI

The Siddhi of your Vocation is the afterglow from the Gift. The Gift is where your work lies. The Gift is where you have to take the leap of initiative into the unknown. The challenge of the Gift is that it keeps on demanding you take these leaps. It is not enough just to take a single leap, and then sit back on your laurels. Your Vocation is constantly drawing you beyond your comfort zone into greater expansion of consciousness. As you expand, it appears that more and more possibilities open up to you. As the siddhic frequency becomes aware of itself, your horizon opens up exponentially. This demands even greater clarity of awareness since you can only steer a single course in life. There will be paths that open to you that you will have to therefore decline from taking.

It is very easy to get carried away by the energies of the higher frequencies and their opportunities. Our tendency is to get caught by the external opportunities that come our way, and become enmeshed in the ensuing drama. Threading your way through this expanding phase of your life will demand deep inner focus, and a continuing deepening of simplicity. As life opens up to you in its infinite dimensions, you must learn to respond by simplifying and by focusing on the essential. You may make many mistakes in this, and will learn that they have been an integral part of your learning. The Siddhi is never a goal; rather it is always the underlying essence revealed through learning from the so-called *mistakes* of our lives. The Siddhi is what is left over once our addiction to drama has been exhausted. In this sense the Siddhi is never ahead of us in the future, but hidden deep within the folds of the present.

THE SIX LINES OF YOUR VOCATION

When you look at the Six lines of the Sphere of Vocation, you will only understand them fully if you read them as a whole. These lines are designed to operate harmonically in relationship with each other. All the lines of the Pearl Sequence can be seen in this way. This is a teaching about synarchy - that higher self-organising consciousness that reaches out across the many human gene pools to bring us together in a higher service to the whole. These 6 lines are the structural basis of synarchy, describing our potential collective future - one that can only be brought about when many of us begin to live out our true Vocation. When you read your specific lines you need to bear this in mind - we are not designed to prosper in isolation. That is mistaking wealth for prosperity. Wealth is exclusive. Prosperity is inclusive because it sees beyond selfishness, and looks toward a future in which we all cooperate with each other for the sake of the whole.

Each of the following Keynotes are words that resonate with the contemporary corporate culture. However, they should be understood in their very broadest sense, across many dimensions. Our modern business-oriented worldview is a deeply flawed model that has grown out of the rapid expansion of the world economy, and the model of free trade that had its roots in the Middle Ages. Although the current model may have its advantages, it is unsustainable and therefore ultimately self-destructive. It is highly unlikely that it will therefore survive the coming transition of consciousness. The Pearl Keynotes help us to see how a new world economic model could come into the world through a new understanding of the old paradigm and its language.

To help understand these terms, you will also find 6 other words in parentheses. You will not find these words in your Profile, as they are metaphorical terms that may help you to understand the base keynotes. The analogy, which may be an apt one, comes from the drama and entertainment industry. Each of these lines in parentheses describes a different function of what it takes to bring a play, book, or film out into the world.

Line 1 - Production (the scriptwriter)

There are currently around 7 billion people on our planet. This means that statistically, over 1 billion people have a 1st line Vocation. These people are the midwives of our common future. It is through the 1st line that new impulses and initiatives enter the world. This does not obviously mean that if you do not have a 1st line Vocation that you are not creative. However, there have always been people whose role is to give birth to new inventions, new approaches, and new paradigms. The business of the other 5 lines is to identify, refine, and organise such incentives so that they can be of service to the whole.

If you have a 1st line Vocation, you are in the purest sense a channel for the creative evolutionary impulse. Your strength is in your creativity. However, of the 1 billion + people who have this 1st line, it is likely that very few of them are actually living out their true creative Vocation. It takes courage to break new ground. It takes dedication, focus, and periods of sustained aloneness, as well as a lot of self-doubt to become a true creator. If you have a 1st line Vocation, then apply it to the theme of the Gene Key of this Sphere, and you will instantly see in which domain your creativity lies. You are here to create something that carries this Gift and Siddhi out into the world to others.

In the analogy of drama, the 1st line is the scriptwriter - the one who hatches the idea. However, it is one thing to have the idea, but quite another to bring it into form. This is the difference between genius and non genius - genius is about implementation, hard work, and dedication. To write a great script, you have to throw yourself into the work. You have to live inside the idea. You have to define it, refine it, and polish it until it shines. Every 1st line in this sense is a transmission holder. They have a responsibility to bring through a creative impulse whose higher purpose is to serve the whole, and then they have to move their ego to one side in order for this to occur.

The greatest challenge for the 1st line is realising their limitation and finding the right allies to help bring their transmission into the world. This requires surrender. You have no idea how the idea will be reshaped or received. This part of the process is out of your hands. Your job is simply to write the script, and then place yourself in service of its message. As a 1st line, your gifts do not lie in the domain of marketing, publicity, strategy, sales, or vision. Once you have been true to the heart of your message, most of your job is done. The rest is up to those with whom you forge an alliance. Production means that you are simply the assemby line for an idea, for a new form to emerge into the world. How freeing it can be to know what you are here to do, and what you are not here to do!

Line 2 - Marketing (the agent)

The 2nd line keynote in the Sphere of Vocation is Marketing. Now you have come all this way along the Golden Path, you may have a good sense of the 2nd line. Perhaps you can see why it would be adept at marketing. It is passionate, relationship-based, brilliant, and sometimes provocative, as well as fluid and responsive. The 2nd line builds up a web of contacts and one-to-one relationships that allow it to have an unprecedented impact in the world. Whereas the 1st line has to work hard to dig down a strong foundation, the 2nd line is all about effortlessness. Marketing is about guiding the flow of information into the world. It is important not to take the word *marketing* as literal in this instance. It is figurative, and can be understood best at an archetypal level.

The Vocation of the 2nd line involves and revolves around specific relationships. When a 2nd line follows their true love in life, they will often find themselves drawn to a 1st line person. This is a naturally passionate and symbiotic relationship. An example might be the relationship between the creator and the agent, or the artist and the muse. The 2nd line can help temper the rawness of the 1st line, refining it and steering it. They can also keep the 1st line from becoming self obsessed, bringing them out of the darkness into the world. And this does not have to be a literal relationship. It could be that a 2nd line Vocation is to shine light on a great idea from the past, an idea or person that has a certain purity to it. The 2nd line Vocation is always looking for this pure message or transmission. They are the dancer looking for the right dance, or the virtuoso looking for the right composer.

We humans do not always easily work together. This is one of the reasons why the Pearl follows the Venus Sequence. Once you have purified your own heart, and weeded some of your wounds, then you are ready to be put to work for the universe. We are simply not designed to do everything. There are certainly people who have many gifts, but the essence of prosperity is relatedness - it is about working creatively in union with others - with your soul group or *fractal*. In relationship terms, your fractal refers to those people who you are karmically drawn to work with in life. When you come together with a pure heart, owning and being responsible for your own issues and wounds, then there is a very real chance of something magical occurring in your life.

The 2nd line agent is a genetic karmic connector. They grease the wheels of prosperity through connecting the right people with the right ideas. If you have a 2nd line Vocation, there is nothing more exciting than when you find an idea, or a product, or a person worth guiding out of obscurity into the light. You are always looking for that pure transmission that you sense will have the maximum beneficial impact on the world. It has to be something you feel impassioned about, and that fills you with life. It will also be a challenge at times, because you are pitted against the collective Shadow consciousness, but as a 2nd line, that is why you live - to dance with the devil and to outwit the enemy - not because you crave recognition, but simply because you love the thrill of the ride!

Line 3 - Strategy (the producer)

In business, the most potentially successful of all the lines is the 3rd line. Since it can be addictive at the Shadow frequency, the 3rd line can easily turn into the wealth-obsessed workaholic. It is highly probable that most of the wealthiest men and women in the world either have an abundance of 3rd lines in their Profile, or they have a 3rd line Vocation. Of course, we have learned already that wealth is not the same as prosperity. Wealth can take a heavy toll on your personal life, your deeper sense of spiritual fulfilment, and therefore your physical, emotional, and mental health. When you look at the lives of the very wealthy, it is always fascinating to note how so many of them are still engaged in making more money, even though there is no higher purpose behind it. For many, money becomes an addiction.

At a higher frequency, the 3rd line will use its prodigious talent and energy to serve a higher purpose, and this can be deeply fulfilling for them. These people are the original Robin Hoods - they have the ability to drive any project towards success through their ability to align with current and future trends. But they also have a natural tendency to want to help those in need - so they can make a lot of money and then ensure it helps empower and awaken others. The 3rd line gift is strategy - the innate ability to assess, plan, and implement a direction that is in alignment with universal forces. The 3rd line also has the gift of learning through self-discovery, so they grow in wisdom and *savvy* as they mature. One of the sharpest gifts of the 3rd line is to help people and projects to become more streamlined and efficient. This sometimes means that old modes of thinking have to be updated or sometimes simply thrown out.

If you have a 3rd line Vocation, then you belong in the mainstream culture. You need to move among people, eating and drinking with them, so that you are always in tune with the pulse of the status quo. You are likely to thrive the most either in a group context, or in an urban environment where life is concentrated. In our metaphor, you are like the producer of the movie.

It is your job to take on the responsibility of the whole project. The agent may put you in touch with the scriptwriter, but it is you who has to become the hub of the whole project and the community of people who are needed to bring it to fruition. Your gift will always be to know all the levels and layers of the project, from the writer to the actors to the investors to the director. You are the meat in the pie, and although you may well have the most complex role and may work the hardest, facing many challenges, you will also be one of the most recognised and rewarded for your host of startling skills.

Line 4 - Sales (Director)

Throughout the Golden Path Program we have gotten to know the 4th line as the great 'friendmaker'. This gift comes from a truly genuine heart, and an easy warmth with people and community. This is the kind of person that emerges through the Venus Sequence, as those 4th lines release some of their inner restrictions and fears. To have a 4th line Vocation is to be a spokesperson. Such gifts are given to us to serve the whole, and although the 4th line wound may feel reluctant to engage at this level, they do have to overcome the fear that they inherited in their very early years. When we say that the 4th line is the most natural salesperson of all the lines, it does not mean only in business. The open 4th line is always selling their heart. They are here to create more openness, to help others overcome their fears, and to be examples of open-hearted communication.

Like the 4th line, the 3rd line can be hugely successful in a business context. However, the role and style of the 4th line is very different. Their role is more like the director of the movie. They have to work closely with people, which involves diplomacy, conviction, and focus. The 4th line knows what the movie should look like, and their one-pointed drive will ensure that everyone else comes into harmony around that direction. The 4th line is comfortable taking control and guiding others to work towards a collective vision or ideal.

This is where the notion of sales comes in - the 4th line can diffuse difficulties through the sheer strength and goodwill of its character. The 4th line also has a strong theme of aloneness as a counterbalance to its communal warmth. The inner strength and commitment of these people is rooted in this ability to stand alone and remain committed to one's ideal, despite the odds.

If you have a 4th line Vocation, then you are here to influence humanity. You are here to use your considerable gifts to open people's hearts. If you happen to be selling a specific idea or product, then at the deepest level it is really an excuse to share your spirit with others. Sometimes you may also be here to deliver a rousing message that shakes people out of their comfort zones, and brings them to a new place inside themselves. Since the 4th line is so good at convincing people about things, it is for a very good reason. When this reason is for a higher purpose, then your whole life moves onto a higher level. There is nothing more powerful or authentic than when one of us stands alone in the world and expresses the love in our heart - whatever creative form that may take.

Line 5 - Management (the promoter)

Perhaps you are already beginning to have a sense of how these 6 lines of the Sphere of Vocation are designed to collude together. When we break them down into their metaphorical counterparts like this, it helps us to see how like a jigsaw puzzle we humans really are. We are designed to interlock and work together, sharing skills and resources in order to bring about collective prosperity. You can see how modern business has come together around these ideas, but with one vital difference - those at the top of the hierarchy are primarily interested in creating wealth. It is perhaps strange that most modern businesses do not really ask themselves the most fundamental business question: why are we in business? If they do ask this question, then often it is not in enough depth. If the answer is to make money, then the answer is unsustainable.

It is the 5th line, working in conjunction with the 6th line, that has the capacity to completely transform our world. In the global synarchy, the 5th line represents the management. There always has to be someone in charge, but the golden question is the same one Perceval asks of the Holy Grail: who are you truly in service to? If we put ourselves before the whole, then our entire approach becomes unsustainable. This is the foundation of our modern economic model. We have consistently seen the 5th line as the archetype of the leader throughout this Golden Path Program, and the leader carries a heavy responsibility on their shoulders. The weight of the future therefore depends upon those with 5th lines in their Profile, and in particular those with a 5th line Vocation.

If you have a 5th line Vocation then you have the opportunity to be one of the heralds of the new global consciousness, at whatever level you play within the whole. You must ask yourself the Grail Question: what is the highest service I can perform for my fellow human beings and the earth? In my short lifespan, what is the most I can do? The answer for you must then be transmitted to others and brought to as many people as possible. In the modern internet age, the 5th line has arrived at the age in which it can achieve its zenith. You can reach so many people across the world in such a short space of time. When the 5th lines come together at a much higher frequency then they will begin to change not just the way in which we do business, but the reason why we do business. For a business to be in service of the whole, then its whole structure must be different. It must be a cohesively run organism whose players all have the same vision at their hearts. This is not just an idealistic dream, but a real possibility. Commerce can become a sacred means of serving ourselves and the world. We just have to begin it in a new way. With their practical abilities, the 5th line carries the potential to make this dream real.

As the promoter of a new ideal, the 5th line's role is to oversee the whole project, and work out how best to deliver it to the world. They alone are answerable for the success or failure of any endeavour. If the 5th line is heavy-handed in their leadership style, then they will create friction and resistance within the organism. The high frequency 5th line knows that nature itself is most efficient, when it has the freedom to self-organise. This means that governance needs a very deep understanding combined with a light touch. Leadership based on virtue and humility is the most powerful form of governance. It is a very exciting time for the 5th line to be alive, because it is a time for smashing old paradigms, and innovating an entirely new structure and language that can maximise the amazing creative genius inherent in the human race.

Line 6 - Philanthropy (the investor)

The 6th line, as always, stands apart from the other 5 lines. This does not make such people any more special than anyone else. If anything, their life and role is more challenging. This is because the 6th line represents a future ideal that has still not fully come into the world. In the case of the Sphere of Vocation, the role of the philanthropist is still very marginal in the modern world. Today we think of philanthropy as the luxury of the wealthy, rather than seeing it as a worldview that might one day be espoused by everyone. Philanthropy is also greatly misunderstood. As the hub of the Pearl teachings and transmission, philanthropy refers to the investment of energy, time, and/or money into an area where it will do the maximum amount of good. This is different from charity, which can be understood as a general sense of goodwill and service aimed at those who are suffering.

Philanthropy is about seeing the long-term view. In passing a homeless person on the street, the charitable person may give them some money, or even a meal. The philanthropist might appear to pass them by, but be disturbed enough to find a way to help alleviate the whole culture that leads to homelessness.

The 6th line is therefore the ultimate investor. They consider the Grail Question constantly: what is the purpose of our business? What is the use of financial success, if we do not serve a vision beyond ourselves and beyond our current generation? The 6th lines of the world may well feel as though they hardly yet belong in a world where the higher purpose of prosperity still goes unquestioned.

However, the time of the 6th line is fast approaching. Because the 6th line is not involved in the mechanics of the process of making money, they are able to hold the vision of where we are going. One day every company, every community, and every country will have a 6th line department, and that department will steer the whole underlying direction of the many endeavours that we humans are involved in. The 6th line department is rooted in a vision and understanding of sustainability, where the money made is continually ploughed back into the earth, and given to those projects and people who uphold the highest values. An economic model based upon the 6th line view would look entirely different from the current system. Competition would be used positively - not as a means to create more wealth for a few individuals, but as a means of doing the greatest amount of good.

You may feel that such an outlook is idealistic and unrealistic on reading the above words, but if you have a 6th line Vocation and your heart is reopening after a long sleep, then you will probably resonate strongly with this worldview. We do not know what will happen to the current world economy. We do know that it is unsustainable, which suggests that at a certain stage it will collapse. Before that occurs, the 6th lines of the world will need to work together with all the other lines to bring a new model into the world - and one that is based upon the highest values of service to the whole. This model is known as synarchy. As the investor in the movie, the 6th line does not get to influence the outcome of the movie or the way in which it is implemented. The only control that the 6th line has, is in choosing who and what to invest in. And as we will see, that is the ultimate control.

In the world that is coming, the 6th lines will take the initiative to act on their ideals, and in doing so they will karmically attract the teams and fractals of people who will come together to achieve remarkable feats. The 6th line knows the great secret of nature - that generosity is the most potent force in the universe. As the Grail legend testifies, it is the only quality that can even outshine Grace.

CONTEMPLATING YOUR VOCATION - REDEFINING YOUR ROLE

The purpose of your Pearl Sequence is to bring to crystal clear clarity about what you are really here to do in life. This wisdom allows you to continue to contemplate your life in the material dimension, bringing the spiritual dimension in underneath. Ask yourself the Grail Question over and over again: how can I be of the utmost service to the world in the short time that I am alive? Look at your Gene Keys and their lines for insights to help you see a clear answer. The answer you are looking for will come as an insight that opens up in your whole being, rather than just an intellectual answer. You need to continually remember that the Pearl is about prosperity through simplicity. The answer is so simple it is usually staring us in the face. We just have to be bold enough to see it.

THE PEARL AND THE OYSTER - EMBODYING PROSPERITY

The Gene Keys Golden Path is full of wonderful metaphors, stories, and allegories. The transmission of the Pearl also has another dimension that we must consider - that of embodiment. How do we actually embody the feeling of prosperity? If we can feel it inside our physical body, then it will begin to radiate outwards into our life. This is a practical aid to our physical contemplation. Every pearl is grown within an oyster in an organic process involving the elements of earth, air, and water. The oyster therefore represents the body, the shell in which the living gem of prosperity is nurtured, grown, and polished. Each stage and Sphere of the Pearl teaching also includes a journey into an aspect of our physical body and its structure.

The other beauty of the Pearl as a metaphor is that the Pearl itself grows around a microscopic irritation or aberration within the shell. In the same way, we humans are here to unlock the Gifts within our Shadows. Nowhere is this truer than in the Sphere of our Vocation, which we will recall from the Venus Sequence, is also the Sphere of our Core Wound. The Gene Keys teachings are rooted in this notion of physical embodiment, in which our contemplation becomes progressively deeper until it triggers our hearts to open. As your contemplation hits its zenith in the Pearl, you may experience great inner clarity, as the transmission begins to help you tune into your essence.

VOCATION, INITIATIVE, AND THE SPINE - STRENGTH AND FLEXIBILITY

As you contemplate the Sphere of your Vocation, you might like to bring your awareness into your spine. Your spinal column is the first place where you can begin to tune into the prosperity of life within you. Your spine is the power column that carries you through the world. It governs all your movements and micromovements, from standing to walking to running. As you empower yourself to fulfill your unique path to prosperity, so you will awaken the power of your spine. You will walk more tall, you will feel physically stronger, emotionally calmer, and mentally clearer. Your spine dictates how you meet the world. A healthy spine aligns your subtle bodies, it deepens your breathing, and helps you feel capable of dealing with any challenge life throws at you.

The beauty of your spine is that it combines strength with flexibility and firmness with flow. As you contemplate your Vocation, keep bringing your awareness back into your spine. Feel the currents of prosperity flowing through your central nervous system, feeding your brain, softening your heart, and aligning you with your highest destiny.

4. THE SPHERE OF CULTURE

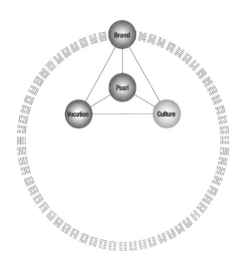

THE SPHERE OF YOUR CULTURE - BUILDING YOUR FRACTAL LINE

Once again in looking at the Pearl Sequence, we can compare it to the Activation Sequence with its 3 themes of challenge, breakthrough, and core stability. In the Pearl, the challenge is reflected in the first Pathway of Initiative, the breakthrough in the second Pathway of Growth, and the core stability in the third Pathway of Service. We have seen what a challenge it is to take the initiative in life - to risk our hearts and dreams out in the wild and unpredictable world. And yet the reward of meeting this challenge is the breakthrough of growth. Your courage stirs the forces of evolution, and opens you up to greater possibilities through the Sphere of your Culture.

The Sphere of your Culture opens or closes you to calling in and building your 'fractal line' - the group of like-minded, open-hearted companions and allies who will aid you in fulfilling your external purpose in the world. As you answer the inner calling of your Vocation, so you send out a message into the cosmos that you are ready for action! One of the most scintillating mysteries of life is that the moment you take the leap, others in your fractal line also do the same. The following comes from the Glossary of Personal Empowerment at the back of the Gene Keys book:

Fractal Line — When our current universe was conceived at the moment of the Big Bang, the crystalline seed of our evolution shattered into countless fractal shards or fragments. These fractal aspects of the whole radiated out in precise geometric patterns known as fractal lines. All fractal lines can be traced back to one of three primary fractal lines, thus seeding the trinity within all aspects of the holographic universe. As you move into deeper harmony with your true nature, you come into alignment with all beings within your seed fractal line, which catalyses great synchronicity and grace in your life.

From the *Glossary of Personal Empowerment*

We humans have always wondered about the workings of fate. What is it that governs the forces of good and bad fortune? Why do some people just appear to be lucky and others not? These are deep and mysterious questions. The Pearl transmission directly engages with these questions, not as a philosophical enquiry, but as a living involvement. By letting your heart dictate your sense of initiative, you will set forces in motion that lay the foundation for prosperity to occur. Of course, this cannot be faked. You must do the heart-work first before your mind becomes clear enough to see what it is you are here to do. It is all too easy to mistake emotional enthusiasm for our heart, and then we rush into something unready and unprepared, and the fractal line will be faulty and weak, inevitably leading to disappointment and chaos.

THE LUCIDITY OF THE WATER EYE

Your Pearl Sequence will not fully engage in your life until you have moved through your Venus Sequence. The Venus work can take some time and dedication. Much depends on your ability to reawaken your self-love and accept and embrace the mental, emotional, and physical obstacles of your early conditioning. You also need to heed the warnings in the Venus Sequence about becoming overly 'bogged down' in your wounding. You will always know when the Pearl is coming alive inside your life, because you will find your mind becoming much clearer and more lucid. In the introduction of this book, we spoke of the Fire Eye and the Water Eye, two very different ways of viewing life. The Fire Eye sees life as pattern and sequence and order, whereas the Water Eye sees at a more visceral and wholesome level, through the whole body.

As the Pearl Sequence opens up in your life, you will become more and more aware of the view through the Water Eye.

You will rely less on the need for answers and facts, and begin to revel in the imagination of life. Through releasing your need to understand everything, you will paradoxically see with crystal-clear eyes. Everything will come into focus in your life.

Things will become more effortless, your mind will slow down, and you will see into the subtle beauties of the world in a way you have never done before. There is no technique to the Pearl Sequence. One can only describe its manifestations. In many ways, the opening of your Pearl Sequence arises as a by-product of the opening of your heart through the Venus Sequence. Although you have to begin by taking the initiative, this sequence is something you may witness occurring in your life, almost in a timeless dimension.

JUPITER AND THE 3 WISE MEN

The Golden Path is an odyssey that unites the earthy truths of our everyday lives with the celestial rhythms of the firmament. Your Hologenetic Profile is calculated from the geometric positions of certain planets in relation to your birth and cycle of gestation. Thus far we have explored the basic duality of the sun and earth through the Activation Sequence, followed by the cyclic and magnetic phases of the moon governing our Attractor Field in the Venus Sequence. The rest of our Venus Sequence consists of the dynamic interplay of the planets Mars and Venus as they interact at the time of our birth, and while we are being imprinted in the womb.

Your Pearl Sequence involves the geometric archetypal relationship of 3 planets; Mars and the Sun seen through a new dimensional lens, joined by Jupiter, which forms the nexus of the Pearl Sequence. You may note that these 3 planets all hold traditionally masculine roles at a mythic level. In their own way they are the 3 wise men in the sky.

Most astrologers might question Mars as a role model for wisdom, and yet Mars as an archetype holds so much potential, just as our Core Wound can one day become our deepest Vocation.

Jupiter however has great importance in our solar system even at a purely astronomical level. Because of its massive size and gravitational pull, it sucks in many of the potentially dangerous celestial objects that pass through our solar system.

In the Pearl Sequence, Jupiter can therefore be seen as a force of great good fortune in our lives. Of course, like all archetypes, Jupiter also has his dark side, which we will see later on.

NATURE AND NURTURE, CULTURE AND CHEMISTRY

At a symbolic level, your Vocation represents nature and your Culture represents nurture. Your Vocation is that rare genius that was imprinted at the moment of your conception. It is the genetic recipe for your differentiated genius. The Sphere of your Culture on the other hand describes the environmental relationships that curl around you in response to the activation of your genius. This is a call and response dynamic. The genius of your vocation calls out to the universe through the Pathway of Initiative. It stirs the cosmic soup to respond through the immutable and mysterious law of synchronicity. The Gene Key of your Culture therefore describes your natural role within the theatre of the wider human community. Your Culture is a yin force that draws others towards you, and that draws you towards them. It is a celestial gathering point.

You can see from the Pearl how the forces of nature and nurture are intricately bound up together. Genius is both within us and without us. We begin our journey to prosperity, and others help bring it to fruition. We are not designed to be islands, but are a vibrating single organism karmically destined to come together in order to fulfill a higher purpose. Our higher purpose is both an individual vibration and a communal unifying field.

Through the 6 lines of the Sphere of Culture, you can see the archetypal building blocks of society. These are the fractal links that will one day complete a global synarchy - a unification of humanity at the highest level of frequency.

Just as every relationship has a specific chemistry, so does every group of human beings. Group chemistry also has a highly specific dynamic that is dependent on the number of people in that group. Every group has a celestial geometry - a group of 3 people has a specific purpose and power within the whole, as does a group of 4 or 5 or 25 or any number. Within larger networks, we can therefore see the fractal nature of group chemistry at work - for example, a larger group of 25 may also consist of several sub-groups of smaller sizes, each with their own geometry. The fabric of human consciousness is like a tapestry woven from many colours, patterns, and strands. At its highest level, this is the principle known as Synarchy.

Synarchy — *The universal principle through which collective intelligence naturally aligns itself in perfect harmony with all that is. Synarchy is the underlying nature of humanity that can only be known once it has emerged from the Shadow frequencies. As the new collective consciousness dawns all across our planet, humanity will self-organise its creative genius and manifest the true higher purpose hidden in its DNA — to bring about the New Eden. Whereas the Shadow consciousness manifests on the material plane through the principle of hierarchy, and the Gift consciousness through the principle of heterarchy, the siddhic consciousness manifests though the principle of synarchy.*

From the *Glossary of Personal Empowerment*

We do not need to understand how group consciousness operates. It is complex beyond measure. We simply need to know where we belong, and find our home within the whole. When each individual does what they love, and what they are designed for (which are one and the same), then the result is effortlessness and harmony. When you are contemplating the Gene Key and line of the Sphere of your Culture, focus your attention on the inner role you are here to play. Where do you fit into the human fractal jigsaw puzzle? Your inner role is how you contribute to the group aura. It is more about the essence that you bring to the group - the Gift and the Siddhi that you emanate - rather than any specific outer skills.

Synchronicity is the glue that places you into context. It is how the universe wheels around you and serves you. As you serve the universe, so it serves you.

THE SHADOW

The Shadow of the Gene Key of your Culture describes a force that directly blocks prosperity from flowing into your life. If there is any point within the whole Golden Path that can free up the flow of money and good fortune in your life, it is this Sphere. Having said this, it is possible (as we will see when we contemplate the Pathway of Growth) to open this point without having first opened our heart in the Venus Sequence. It is relatively easy to make money in life. Many have done so and continue to do so, but at what cost to their health, environment, and deep fulfilment? Money does not make anyone any happier. Even so, you can use the Shadow of your Culture as a key to unlock this area of your life. You will of course have to overcome the fear of the Shadow to unlock the Gift. The most important thing for you is to focus on the ideal of service coming from your heart. When you let that power motivate your Vocation, then you will draw in allies operating at a similar frequency.

The Shadow of your Culture contains a dangerous and dark power. This is the dark side of the Jupiter archetype. If you are motivated by fear and/or greed, then the universe will align you with allies of a similar motivation. You may begin a project or endeavour with good intentions, but because you have not done the Venus work of clearing your heart from ancestral pain, your working relationships will eventually collapse. Like all Shadow manifestations, this can of course be a great teaching for us. Truly open-hearted relationships in business are still a rare thing.

THE GIFT

The Gift of your Gene Key in the Sphere of Culture is one of the three 'triggers' along the Golden Path. As with the Sphere of your Evolution in your Activation Sequence, and the Sphere of your IQ in the Venus Sequence, deep contemplation on this Sphere can lead to a swift shattering of a particular limiting pattern.

In the case of the Sphere of Evolution, this is the breakthrough that comes from realising you can accept your suffering instead of resisting it. In the Venus Sequence, an opening in the Sphere of your IQ can trigger a rush of blocked emotion that was held in check by a deep mental belief rooted in a lack of self-worth. Here in the Pearl Sequence, an opening in the Sphere of your Culture can crack open an age-old pattern that has kept you from prospering. This is a shattering of poverty consciousness - that widely held Shadow belief that there is not enough resources for everyone to flourish. The Gift of this Sphere can propel you into a whole new creative phase of life.

When you contemplate the Gene Key and line that corresponds to your Culture, think about how this Gift of yours might fit best into society. What is your role within the orchestra? What is the dream fragment that you carry on behalf of the whole? See yourself as a single diamond facet in a great wheeling plan. You need not try and find this role. Rather you must trust your initiative, and let it magnetise the right forces and allies towards you, at the right time. Contemplating the Gene Keys can be a very powerful spiritual practise, and it can yield potent results. It is even more powerful when you spend some time focusing on a single Gene Key and its line. If you want to see the mystery of synchronicity at work, go deeply into the Shadow, Gift, Siddhi, and line of the Gene Key of your Culture.

THE SIDDHI

It is interesting to note how our inner definition of prosperity changes as we move from the Gift frequency to the Siddhi. The Siddhi represents our innermost essence, therefore it always has a deep inward focus. Unlike the Gift, which belongs in the outer world through its beautiful creative outpouring, the Siddhi flowers as we lose interest in outer prosperity. This must be understood very clearly or you may misunderstand this teaching. Creativity is the heart of a well-lived human life, and creativity that comes from your core always leads to inner and outer prosperity.

The difference between the Siddhi and the Gift is that the Siddhi of your Culture is primarily absorbed by the practise of philanthropy. What the Gift earns, the Siddhi wants to give away. In this, you cannot jump right to the Siddhi, but must travel through the journey that emerges from the Gift.

The Siddhi of the Sphere of Culture represents a simplifying of your life. For this Siddhi to burn brighter in your consciousness, you must come naturally into the deep love of simplicity. This is why so many true sages have given away their possessions. This is not to say you should do the same, but it does suggest that as the lucidity of our awareness blooms, so our priorities in life naturally begin to change. The form this takes will vary greatly from person to person. The key to any such transformation is first to embrace the Gift and go out into the world, and be a part of something beautiful and creative.

THE SIX LINES OF YOUR CULTURE

The 6 lines of the Sphere of Culture offer a profound insight into the lines themselves. Once you have understood these 6 lines, you can train them upon any of the Spheres that make up your Golden Path. This is always an interesting thing to do as we imbibe the progressive wisdom of the 6 lines. Each layer of keynotes brings depth and richness to your understanding of all your lines as well as broadening the scope of your contemplation. You are strongly recommended to read the entire section below as it tells the story of how the lines all intersect, how they have evolved through history, and where they are going in terms of their highest potential.

Line 1 - Individual

The 1st line is essentially about the individual. This does not necessarily mean that it is selfish, though it may well be self-absorbed. The 1st line is self-motivated, and in the widest sense this means that it is an entrepreneur. The entrepreneur sets out in the world as a solo player armed only with their ideal, and the impulse to propagate it. If you have a 1st line Culture, then you are a wellspring of something completely new. This will take a great deal of courage, because much of our conditioning tells us to follow others and 'fit in'. The 1st line will have to stand alone in the world with their ideal. They will have to expose themselves to risk, perhaps to ridicule, and certainly to criticism. However, the beauty of entrepreneurship is that if your ideal is true, very soon you will draw support and recognition from all manner of unexpected directions. As you keep standing behind your ideal, you will watch a fractal organism gradually forming itself around you. This is the miracle of following your Vocation and taking the Initiative. Allies will keep on appearing with the skills and enthusiasm to help you in manifesting your dream.

The individual is the core unit of the Synarchy. Synarchy is an omnicentric organism, and even though it forms itself into teams, networks, and gene pools, its strength always derives from the individual. In a synarchy, it is always the 1st lines who emanate the initiatives and ideas that will allow the synarchy to gather. The transmutation of collective consciousness has to begin somewhere with someone. If you have a 1st line Culture, then you carry a great responsibility to stand alone with your dream, and call out to the collective to gather around a higher ideal. You are that cosmic, karmic rallying point. When we look into history, we often see that the greatest breakthroughs were made by people who were so far ahead of their time that they went largely unrecognised in their own age. This can be the case with the 1st line, but it need not worry them.

Prosperity does not always require recognition. It is a feeling of deep inner fulfilment that transcends outer conditions. The beauty of synarchy is that even though the ideal may have begun with you, it very soon surpasses you as others join you, and the dream takes a greater hold, and begins a life of its own. At a certain point in your evolution as a 1st line, you will therefore have to let go of thinking that it was your idea, and that you have any more importance than anyone else in the jigsaw. When a 1st line attains this realisation then their work in the world is essentially done. This is however a huge step for the human ego to take - to bring something so precious into the world, and then to step back and let it go. Your role as the 1st line is to gestate the dream inside you, and then to bring it into the world. Where it goes and how it changes once it is in the world, is no longer in your hands.

Having said all the above, the 1st line often does get great recognition. This is why it can be hard for them to let go of control, because recognition can so easily lead to inner confusion. If the 1st line really looks deep inside themselves, they may realise that although recognition can feel wonderful, it is never the goal. It is simply the perfume of their dream reaching out into the synarchy, and it goes as swiftly as it comes. The real love of the 1st line is never the result, but the mystery of the creative process itself.

Line 2 - Partnership

Each of the 6 lines of the Sphere of Culture brings with it an inner initiation. The links of a higher collective consciousness demand that we transcend our Shadow tendency to cling to the familiar. The 2nd line is the great link of partnership. Partnership has many dimensions to it - the ultimate human partnership is our partnership with the earth and its rhythms, elements, and creatures. On a more microcosmic scale, partnership is the next unit of scale in collective consciousness after the individual. This is human partnership, which is about 2 people coming together in order to manifest something in the world. In business, partnership is a common phenomenon, because at a high frequency it strengthens resources, pools talent, and offers dynamic support and inspiration for any endeavour.

If you have a 2nd line Culture, then you are designed to thrive in partnership. The 2nd line comes alive when the chemistry is right, when their gifts are recognised, and when they recognise the gifts of others. The secret to 2nd line success is therefore entirely dependent on frequency. You will draw towards you those partnerships that reflect your capacity.

If you compromise your Gifts, then your partnership will never feel balanced, and will breed resentment and eventual crisis. If you are a 2nd line Culture, you operate at your best in one-to-one situations. This doesn't mean that you aren't a team player, but it does mean that this is the way you fit best within a team. Your partner can be someone either with less or more responsibility than you in the synarchy. This is not about leadership - it is about the mutual exchange of respect, talent, and character. The 2nd line thrives on complementarity, and gets on best when the chemistry of the partnership is dynamic yet balanced, so that the 2nd line passion is in no way stymied.

A 2nd line partnership can be anything from 2 people who are actually married, to an executive and their personal assistant (the 2nd line can be either role). There are so many situations in the world in which 2 people become interdependent allies. And the 2nd line Culture also comes with its challenges - these might be over-reliance on the relationship, attachment to the external roles of the relationship leading to jealousy, confusion over sexuality, or just too much intensity.

The 2nd line therefore really has its work cut out to transcend the outer appearance of the partnership, and rise above the many pitfalls of the Shadow consciousness. For a 2nd line partnership to remain clear, it must be founded upon some form of mutual higher vision or service. Only if the partnership is in service to something greater than itself, can it keep free from the Shadow frequencies.

One key for the 2nd line Culture is to cultivate more than one partnership in life (this does not obviously apply within the realm of intimate relationships!).

As a 2nd line Culture, you will be the bridge into many different spheres and communities through the key partnerships that you naturally form throughout your life. There will always be people who you are immediately drawn towards, and who are drawn towards you. Having said this, you are not like the 4th line, whose inherent affability can make friends anywhere. Your relationships are much more specific, and even perhaps more specialised since they form around your mutual passion, whatever that is. All of this gives the 2nd line a unique higher role to play within the planetary synarchy.

Line 3 - Unit

In order for collective consciousness to awaken on our planet, first of all the individual must transcend their own suffering through deep acceptance of the wound. Out of this deep self-love emerges the possibility for a new kind of sacred relationship. As 2 energies combine for a mutual higher purpose, they generate an auric field that has extraordinary capacity for manifestation. The next scale of collective consciousness is the unit. The unit is the archetypal ideal of the human family. But family here refers to far more than just genetic relationship. True family occurs whenever 3 or more human beings come together for a higher purpose. The power of sacred partnership is that it has the capacity to form a higher kind of family - the fractal family. The fractal family is a small, highly cohesive unit of individuals who share the same higher ideal, but whose Gifts can be interwoven in such a way that they can manifest the birth of that ideal.

The unit consists of between 3 and 15 members. When more than 15 individuals come together, then you have the beginnings of a network (the theme of line 4). In modern business this equates to the small business or enterprise, or the unit can also thrive as a department or specific team within a larger organism.

If you have a 3rd line Culture then you will thrive in a small group setting. The 3rd line comes alive through diversity, dynamism, and exchange of ideas and opinions. The 3rd line does not need consensus, but recognises that conflict can be very creative if the members of the group are able to work through a process of self-transcendence. The dynamics of a creative group aura require flexibility, patience, wisdom, and a very good sense of humour. All these are key attributes of the 3rd line Culture.

If you have a 3rd line Culture, then true prosperity for you is more about excitement and interaction than any result. You prosper in the process, and the result or reward is simply a by-product. The 3rd line Culture belongs right in the heart of civilisation, at the cutting edge where wider social change can be implemented in the world. The unit is unique in that it is right in the centre of the synarchy, so it has a responsibility to convert the ideals and transmissions of lines 1 and 2 into strategies that can then be rolled into the networks and societies of lines 4 and 5.

In contemplating the Sphere of your Culture, you need to consider the nature of the Gift and Siddhi of the Gene Key you have, and then intuit how it might emerge through your line theme. The 3rd lines are often best at understanding how the principle of synarchy really operates at a grass roots level. It can be infinitely complex when viewed through the mind, but when you grasp it intuitively, it seems suddenly so very, very simple. The 3rd line Culture therefore knows the mechanics of manifestation at a very deep level within their DNA. The 3rd line is also well suited to molding and shaping human chemistry, so that it operates at its highest efficiency.

Perhaps more than any other line, the 3rd line understands the universal law that any group is far more than the sum of its parts. Every group has a living chemistry, and the 3rd line Culture is adept at getting the very best out of that chemistry. In this sense they can be an extraordinary force for good.

Line 4 - Network

You may by now be realising that the principle of synarchy is made up of fractal, scaleable units. The first 3 lines of the Sphere of Culture describe the building blocks of civilisation - individuals, relationships, and families. On a business level, this translates as sole traders, partnerships, and small businesses. The greater percentage of all world businesses are in fact small businesses, and usually family businesses. Until the last century and the dawn of the industrial age, anything larger than this was always the domain of the monarchy or the ruling elite. The 4th, 5th and 6th lines have therefore always been firmly entrenched in the old hierarchical model. In fact as we shall see, the 6th line has never really existed other than as an intuited higher power - a God or many gods. The world we see around us today with its vast interlinked global economy is therefore the very early manifestation of the higher potential of the 4th and 5th lines. However, despite the progress of civilisation, the old model still holds us back. It is as though the world has changed, but we have not yet caught up with it.

As a higher octave of the 1st line, the 4th line is the primary building block of collective consciousness. The network is quite literally a neural net made up of line 1's, 2's, and 3's. The advent of the internet obviously allows us to join together in ways we have never previously dreamed of. The 4th line therefore requires a new kind of thinking - 'synthinking'. Synthinking is an intuitive way of using logic that can see and map the holographic patterns behind evolution. Many of the younger generations are literally trained to think in this new way by the new technologies that continue to emerge.

Synthinking is not exclusive to the 4th line, but it does appear to be a specialisation of the 4th line. It involves the rewiring of the two hemispheres of the brain, so that they come into a higher harmony. The 4th line can recognise the 'fractal lines' that connect people and places, and is highly attuned to the synchronicity at work behind the events of our lives.

If you have a 4th line Culture, then you are a pioneer in making use of the connectivity of our modern culture. Through their inherent resonance with community, all 4th lines hold the key to our future collective consciousness. However, the 4th line first has to overcome its own inner obstacles - its tendency to isolate itself, its potential lack of boundaries in relationships (these last 2 are ever-connected), and its fear of the responsibility of its position in the global synarchy. As a 4th line you have only to re-open your heart, and your life will explode into bloom in ways you can hardly imagine. Your role is to bridge different spheres and networks. This can be about bringing together different gene pools, different skills, different ideas, and different cultures. You are a synthesiser, an alchemist who works with life's polarities and opposites, combining and recombining them in new and novel ways.

In working as a conduit for collective consciousness, the 4th line has to learn to stay rooted in its own culture, while at the same time expanding outwards to embrace other cultures and the many-layered strata of society. The 4th line must therefore learn many languages - not literally - but figuratively - the language of different networks, cultures, customs, and beliefs. They have to be open to the poor and the wealthy in equal measure, sometimes being the bridge for the two to come together. They have to stretch their own identity to encompass all manner of new ideas, and in doing so they will be forever changed. This is why the 4th line must have a strong sense of its own individuality and roots, as a counterbalance to its pervasive and expansive worldview.

When you are contemplating the Gene Key of your Culture, think about the many ways in which this quality can be spread throughout you and those other cultures and sub-cultures that you will move through.

Line 5 - Society

When you look back upon human history, you can see the story of the 6 lines writ large. We began with the survival of the fittest, the individual quest for brute survival, then came the realisation that lasting partnerships gave us and our genes a better chance of survival, so we naturally formed into small groups and families. These families in time became tribes and gene pools with their own customs and languages. At a certain point, there was a great change that swept through humanity, and this came with the birth of agriculture. As we moved away from our hunter-gatherer lifestyle, and began to form larger groups working the land together, so we needed to develop forms of governance. The best model we could come up with at that time of our development was the hierarchical model with a governing elite and a servile majority. This is how the different networks and tribal groupings managed their expanding lifestyle.

The code of life however still has 2 more scaling units left in its genetic database. The 5th line represents something entirely different - a consciousness that first came online as certain individuals realised that they could increase their individual power exponentially. Certain individuals, partnerships, and families that were already in control of large networks organised the first armies, and set out to conquer other networks and tribes. This was the advent of war, which you may recall from the Saturn Sequence, is the mythic wound of the 5th line. War gave way to empire, a good term for the Shadow of the 5th line Culture. We have repeatedly seen the 5th line's gift for leadership, which is based upon practicality and implementation. This gift can be used to serve oneself, or to serve the whole. The bottom line is that the 5th line has this awesome power and ability to just get things done.

The great empires of the past consisted of scores of networks all joined together to form a wider society. Even though these societies may have been forged out of violence (we still see the remnants of this in the world today), these networks in time became the nations and nation states.

The most common place we see the 5th line at work today is in politics and big business, where it continues to lead humanity, for good or for bad. The great corporations and monopolies are the new empires that continue to absorb networks, and grow until they become unwieldy and unsustainable. We can see that the Shadow consciousness continues to drive all the line themes even in our modern times.

However, light is breaking through. Just as the 4th line has this magnificent potential to create a new holographic way of uniting civilisation, the 5th line also has the potential to lead us into a brighter future. With a healed heart, the 5th line no longer seeks power, but is driven by the urge to solve large scale problems. The 5th line loves to solve practical problems (you may recall the 5th line 'fixer' from the Activation Sequence). If you have a 5th line Culture, then you have the capacity to be a global player. Take a good look at the Gift and Siddhi of the Sphere of your Culture, and you will see a capacity for global influence. And when you look at the Shadow, you will see the one quality that may prevent you from assuming this mantle. The 5th line Shadow usually is either too afraid of its own power, or it becomes obsessed by it. Your challenge is to open your heart to your highest potential.

The 5th line can bring to fruition what the 1st line gives birth to. The 5th line needs to make it practical and accessible for everyone. They are the 'promoter' after all. They can organise all the other elements of the synarchy to serve a single higher purpose. It is the 5th line's charisma, love, and generosity of spirit that will help change our world.

The 5th line needs to live a life of action. The 4th line may have the answers, but the 5th line insists on them being put into action.

The 5th line also gathers together all the elements of society - the individuals, partnerships, families, and networks, and recognises their equal importance and responsibility. The power of the 5th line only fully emerges when they serve the greater empire, the ideal of a higher society. This great dream does not belong to a single person or elite group.

It is an omnicentric model of consciousness in which every centre conveys a vital fractal aspect of the whole dream of a new world order. The 5th line therefore has to transcend its own desire for recognition and power, and serve this higher self-organising model. You can see what an exciting time it is for the 5th lines of the world today.

Line 6 - System

In the past, the 6th line was either the domain of the religious authority or the outcast. From birth, the 6th line carries a powerful intuition about the holistic nature of the cosmos, and this sets it apart from the other lines and their processes. This has led to the 6th line often being seen as 'special'. Culture is often cruel to such people, as they engender either fear or awe in others. There is a big difference between the way that the 5th line manifests collectively as religion and the 6th line's mysticism. The former is a social construct using tradition, ritual, and manipulation (conscious or unconscious) to bring the masses together, whereas the 6th line has no real interest in power. The 6th line carries a huge spiritual longing, and this can make them more contemplative but sometimes also more lost in the world. At its worst, the 6th line can be utterly indifferent to the suffering of others, and can commit all manner of atrocities just to try and fill the emptiness they feel inside.

At its best, the 6th line can capture a vision of the mystery of life at the most profound level, and they can feed off this ideal for the rest of their lives. This can make them a magnet for anyone who has even a slight intuition that there is more to life than just everyday survival. The 6th line experiences life at the 'system' level. This is a mysterious term that takes some penetration.

The structure and evolution of human society follows a certain pattern, and although that pattern is hard to see with the logical brain, it can be sensed through our higher faculties. The system refers to the organising principle behind everything. Traditionally, this has been seen as a God or gods. In our modern post-industrial age, the scientific mind is the more common means of trying to interpret and understand life at the system level.

The system is nature itself, which includes us humans, and the way we think and/or believe. To understand the system level of consciousness, you cannot adhere to any single viewpoint. You cannot, for example, be only a scientist or only a religious person. The 6th line is designed to sit right on edge of everything in the witnessing consciousness, observing life from a contemplative perspective. This does not mean that the 6th line is outside of life or society - rather the opposite is true. The 6th line belongs right in the heart and fabric of life, mixing in with all the other 5 lines and their realms and perspectives. In a sense, the 6th line is something of a pretender - they can be everywhere and yet belong nowhere. This is both the strength and sometimes the undoing of the 6th line. If you have a 6th line Culture, you must learn to embrace life and at the same time be a witness to it, and you must be willing to play your role wholeheartedly. In time, your true role will be revealed, but only if you play the game of life with gusto and grace.

In the original I Ching, every hexagram connects to every other hexagram in a sequence. The thread that connects one hexagram to the next is the thread that comes from the sequential unravelling of the 6 lines. It is this thread that connects each 6th line at the end of each hexagram to the 1st line at the beginning of the next hexagram. It is not necessary to understand this in depth, but it holds a secret of the 6th line. In the global synarchy, the 6th line view is always looking to the future, to the next level of our evolution. The great challenge for the 6th line is to be present in their life as it is, while also sensing where life is going.

When we look at the world today, we are only just beginning to see the dawn of collective consciousness - unifying structures like the United Nations, the United States, and the European Union, for all their challenges - are the early versions of a new global unification. The system of nature is always at work behind the scenes - it drives our evolutionary passage towards higher consciousness, even towards a new mutated biology.

For the 6th line Culture, the real challenge is to find a way to be at peace within oneself. You are here to be an embodiment of living wisdom. Your final revelation is that it doesn't matter what you do in life - it doesn't matter what any of us do, it only matters how we do it. This is the root of true prosperity. This simple but profoundest of truths is part of the paradox of the 6th line - to be an actor in the great drama, and to be apart from the drama.

CONTEMPLATING YOUR CULTURE -
FINDING YOUR PLACE WITHIN THE WHOLE

As you contemplate the Gene Key and line of your Culture, you need to realise that this is about surrender. You do not have to find your place within the whole, because the whole will always steer you to the right place. Sometimes we also need to learn through being in the wrong place (although even that is relative). When we pierce the void with the frequency of our Vocation and Initiative, then the universe responds by reorganising our Culture. This is why merely focussing on this Gene Key and its line, can open us up to synchronicity. Prosperity comes through simplicity. This is the entire secret of the Pearl Sequence.

EPIGENETIC PROGRAMMING AND THE ONE POINT

As far as embodiment is concerned, the Sphere of your Culture is about allowing yourself to be mutated by your environment. Whether we like it or not, we humans are programmed by our environment. The science of epigenetics shows us how those around us - our culture and milieu actually program our DNA. The frequency of our responses to our environment dictates the quality of gene transcription in our bodies.

In your physical body, the most powerful junction box is the belly. All the body's major systems can be accessed through the belly. It is in our belly that we digest the frequencies of the world. Whatever frequencies we take in, whether chemical or subatomic, we have the capacity to transform them deep in our core. As you contemplate your Culture, bring your awareness into your belly. Place your hands on your belly regularly. It is here in the one point behind your navel that life finds its centre inside you.

When we have a tense belly, our mind also runs amok, leading us through day after day of unawareness. When we come into our belly, and our breath emerges from our belly, we cannot help but slow down. Our thoughts open out like the clouds parting, and the lucidity of awareness begins to crystalise inside us. We open up to the possibility of breakthrough. We are able to receive life instead of trying to control life. There is no frequency that cannot be transformed into its higher essence inside our belly. This means that there is nothing in the world that we need fear. As your awareness rests more frequently in your belly, so you will find yourself more open to new experiences and surprises. The combination of a strong and tensile spine, and a soft open belly make your life seem like a dance instead of a trial. You can always associate the Gene Key of your Culture and its frequencies with your belly and your navel, and this can lead to some wonderfully deep contemplations and insights.

5. THE PATHWAY OF GROWTH

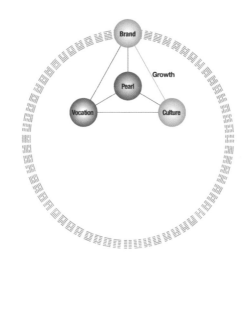

GROWTH - FOR GOOD OR BAD

The 2nd Pathway of the Pearl Sequence is called the Pathway of Growth. In order to fully understand your Pearl Sequence, you need to see the 3 main Pathways of the Pearl Sequence in relationship. Initiative leads to growth, depending on one's Dharma. Sometimes initiative leads to a perceived failure. It all depends on your ability to convert your life experiences into compost that helps you grow in wisdom and understanding. The interesting thing about growth is that it isn't at all dependent on frequency. This means that the Shadow consciousness can make use of this Pathway for its own purposes. Unchecked growth always leads to imbalance, and in nature unchecked growth can overload a system and lead to a crashing of that system. This truth, so easily forgotten by humans - has many implications for our modern world.

GROWING SYNARCHY - ORGANISM V ORGANISATION

The Sphere of Culture and its 6 lines describes a new vision and understanding of the way in which business operates. This new view is called Synarchy, a term mentioned fairly frequently within the Gene Keys text. Synarchy refers to a model of business, education, and governance whose primary purpose is to serve the whole. In business, the prime directive is usually first of all to make money, which may or may not then be used to serve the whole. Synarchy is a reversal of this thinking. When you put the service of the whole first, even before making money, you then engage the entire beneficial force of the universe. This is why the 3rd Pathway in the Pearl Sequence is called the Pathway of Service, and without it there can be no quantum leap. This means sometimes that a business is not supposed to grow beyond a certain point, so that it never turns into an unsustainable wealth-creating machine that just makes money for the sake of making money. We have already seen that prosperity is a flow. It enables you to keep life in perspective by keeping things simple. Many modern businesses end up becoming so large that they swallow resources, and worse still, they swallow people's lives. We were never really intended to live a life where we work for 90% of the time, and have holidays that take up a measly 10% or less. This is a manifestation of an unnatural man-made model.

You don't build a synarchic business. You allow a synarchy to grow. You provide the right elements and conditions and it grows by itself. It is an organism rather than an organisation, and like an organism that is connected to the whole, it is also self-organising. To govern such a model requires a gardener's light touch - you must be able to listen and use your intuition to read the signs that life sends you. Synarchy needs the elements that make up hierarchy, but without the ego. At its core, synarchy always has the beating heart of a higher ideal, and like the bees that all serve the Queen in the hive, the members of a synarchy all serve the ideal in their own unique way.

Growing a business is all about clear vision and clear relationships. Many businesses begin with a high ideal, but then get corrupted by success along the way. As material success rushes through the organism, the members of the business often forget why they began. This is when the ego steps in and tries to steer the organism, making it into a man-made organisation. Without a clear ideal, the organisation is allowed to multiply without check, without question, and the pace of modern business takes over. Often the first thing to occur is the breakdown of relationships, which are now seen as secondary in importance to the business. The business now becomes more complex, requiring more time and people to govern it. Hierarchy takes hold, and with it comes resentment and dominance. We all know the end of this story - it is written large across our planet - we end up serving money, rather than the other way around, and we lose balance, purpose, and above all, we lose perspective.

Initiative + Growth = Wealth - an unsustainable model
Initiative + Growth + Service = Prosperity - a sustainable model

SACRED COMMERCE - A NEW MODEL FOR BUSINESS

To reframe a new model for business, we really need to once again remember the Grail Question mentioned earlier in the Pearl. What is the purpose of business? Whom does it serve? I would like to propose here a rather radical possibility - that business can actually be a path to awakening. Good business is all about connectivity, relationships, sharing resources, and a sense of higher purpose. We have already seen in the Venus Sequence how relationships can be a direct route to awakening, so why not also apply this to the realm of business? In business, we also have to deal with fundamental human issues like fairness, trust, respect, integrity, and transparency. If we view business as a valid spiritual training in its own right, we will find that it holds many hidden opportunities for us to grow, inwardly and externally.

The Pathway of Growth has many dimensions to it. This is as much about spiritual growth as it is material growth. Money can easily occupy a huge amount of our time - either through earning it or worrying about it. It can very easily kill off a whole life without our even noticing until it's too late. One of the secrets of prosperity is therefore to design your business around your lifestyle, rather than letting it dictate your quality of your life. Own first challenge is taking the initiative, and our second is not allowing the results to carry us away. Big success is not for everyone unless you have a strong philanthropic mission from the outset. Small success often makes us happier, because it enables our lives to stay simpler. In life you will see over and over again that the happiest people are those who live relatively simple lives.

Here in the West, we have grown up in a modern world, where it is assumed that happiness is dependent on wealth. Very few people are not taken in by this deep-seated misnomer. Prosperity does not mean that we have to be overly frugal - it means that we maintain a healthy balance between abundance and simplicity. Each person has to work out for themselves what this means and looks like.

For example, someone with a 4th line Culture needs a very different environment from someone with a 2nd line Culture. A simple life is designed out of our awareness, as opposed to a life that we never intended to choose but unconsciously designed nonetheless.

THE RING OF PROSPERITY -
A BLUEPRINT FOR SUSTAINABLE GROWTH

In the Gene Keys pantheon, certain groups or families of Gene Keys form cross-coding chemical and archetypal connections in the human genome. These are the 21 Codon Rings, the programming software responsible for collective behaviour patterns as opposed to individual patterns:

Codon Ring — *A chemical family within your body made up of one or more codons. There are a total of 21 Codon Rings, each one relating to a specific amino acid or stop codon. The Codon Rings are trans-genetic chemical families that operate across entire gene pools, drawing certain people naturally together in pairs, groups, and ultimately forming whole societies. The Codon Rings are the biological machinery behind what the ancients called 'karma'. The manner in which they interlock forms the geometric unified field underpinning humanity, and as human DNA mutates in order to carry the higher frequencies that are coming with the Great Change, the 21 Codon Rings will bring humanity into the biological realisation of its true nature and unity.*

From the *Glossary of Personal Empowerment*

The Codon Ring known as the 'Ring of Prosperity' consists of 2 Gene Keys - the 16th Gene Key and the 45th Gene Key. These two Gene Keys and their Shadows, Gifts, and Siddhis are the codes that ultimately control the balance of poverty and prosperity on our planet. Despite being a small Codon group, they essentially govern the nature of the world economy. This is quite revealing when we look at their Shadows, the 16th Shadow of Indifference and the 45th Shadow of Dominance.

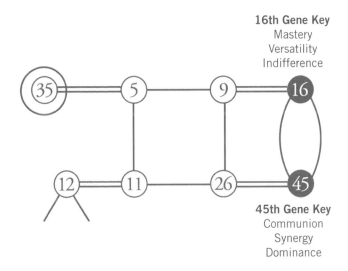

The Codon Ring of Prosperity

In the field of these Shadows, we can see the underlying nature of the old paradigm of hierarchy. Even at its best, the 45th Shadow is driven by tribal loyalty that is immediately suspicious of any other group or community. Out of this fear, the 45th Shadow sets out to dominate others, and expand their territory in order to control the flow of resources. The 16th Shadow on the other hand, manifests as a kind of emotional deadness coupled with a very particular set of skills. The 16th Gene Key has an acute eye for detail, and the ability to build and maintain any system or organisation.

If you were to write a dramatic script out of these two Shadows, they might translate as the power-hungry Regent and the conniving Prime Minister.

These two characters have stalked the world stage for thousands of years. They still operate today under the guise of big business and politics. This culture of indifferent dominance is the underlying nature of the current worldwide business model. We are still competing with each other for dominance, and we still largely neglect the impact this has on our planet as a whole.

Let us look now at the Ring of Prosperity through saner eyes - through its potential creative Gifts. The 45th Gift, having overcome its need to dominate others out of fear, discovers its inherent gift for creating synergy in any group. Synergy is the ability to draw others together, and enthuse and inspire them in such a way that their individual Gifts create a higher energetic field. Synergy elevates the elements of hierarchy into a creative communion. We can imagine how different our world could be, if this were to become the normal business model on a global scale. Humanity has an awesome creative potential to solve its own challenges, and to create a world that is both beautiful and peaceful.

Similarly, the higher frequencies of the 16th Gene Key are about Versatility - the foundation of Synthesis. Currently, our world is full of experts in individual sciences and systems.

The problem with this is that they do not easily understand each other - how can the logician understand the artist and vice versa? The higher Gifts of the 16th Gene Key are the domain of the polymath - the one whose genius spans multiple fields. Once we bring together the understandings of multiple spheres - physics and economics, mysticism and psychology, music and politics, we will finally see the higher view, and we can design a world based on higher evolutionary patterns. The Siddhi of Mastery is built upon the highest use of the qualities of competition, but instead of competing against each other, we compete for individual and group excellence. We compete to see who can be of the greatest service to the whole. This is what happens when Mastery and Communion come together.

6. THE SPHERE OF YOUR BRAND

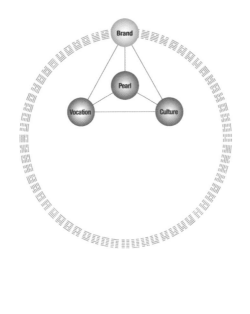

THE BRAND IS YOU

At the apex of the triangle of prosperity that comprises your Pearl Sequence, we find the Sphere of the Brand. The word 'Brand' is derived from an old Saxon word 'Brinnan' meaning both 'to burn' and 'sword'. Your Brand is therefore like your sword - an extension of your spirit that you can wield in the world. We already know this Sphere from the Activation Sequence, where it is known as our Life's Work. One of the mysteries of the Golden Path is that it revisits this Sphere once again towards the end of the journey, but views it through a different lens. Your Brand is the extension of your personality, your outer representation in life. As we also know from the business world, your Brand is your specific stamp or symbol that can catch the attention of others.

Your Brand describes the style and frequency of your outward expression. It comes across in the clothes you wear, the way you talk, and the language you use. Your Brand can be intuited through the way you look and your particular cultural resonance. Your Brand is the platform for the expression of your innermost essence. Because of this, your success in the outer world greatly relies upon you expressing yourself and your higher purpose with clarity and simplicity. When you get your Brand right, then your Life's Work can be expressed effectively and fluidly. Your outer expression will be in exact alignment with your Radiance and Purpose. Every element of your Hologenetic Profile will pulsate in harmony bringing you good fortune and prosperity.

Your Brand is also like a homing beacon that attunes your attractor field to your fractal line. You may recall that your fractal line refers to your true allies in life - your 'soul family'. When you have the courage and initiative to wield your own Brand - your highest truth - then you will draw your true allies into your life. The Pathway of Growth teaches us the importance of this link between our true allies (the Sphere of Culture) and our individual expression (the Sphere of the Brand).

It is important to understand that we are also using the word Brand here in a metaphorical manner - the Brand does not necessarily refer to any set of products or services - in essence, the Brand is You.

EXECUTIVE MAGIC AND THE MARKETING OF TRUTH

At the highest level of frequency, there is only one product, and that product is Truth. In the world there are simply degrees of truth masquerading as products, and we get so attached to buying and selling them all. All of this is the currency of communication that takes place between elements of the one Truth who have forgotten their common source, and therefore feel the need to trade aspects of their own separateness with each other. The world of business and commerce is all a great stage upon which the state of human evolutionary consciousness is made manifest. That we can now see the whole world stage rather than our tiny corner of it, makes the mirror even clearer than ever. As Truth begins to break through into the business world, we will see a slow but sustained transformation moving across the world stage.

One of the first things to be clear about if you are intending on going into business is what your product really is. This may sound very obvious to people, but it may not be so. At the highest level, whatever your physical product is, is not the real product, for as we have said - You are the product. The product and its branding are simply an excuse for you to communicate a frequency down your fractal line. What gets communicated down that line is up to you – it may be fear, greed, desire, love, service, awakening, or any other frequency. The highest frequencies are Truth, Love, and

Awakening, which all amount to the same thing. There is a huge irony if you find yourself in the business of marketing Truth, which is that really you are marketing death! To the separate self in the marketplace, the last thing it wants is to die into its higher nature – which is what happens when one meets Truth. As you may imagine, it is not easy to sell someone their own death, so you have to mask it, and this is where Branding comes in.

The New Age market is filled with all kinds of people peddling all kinds of wares, and making all kinds of claims. Most of the time, these people don't really make any serious money, because they fail to realise that they are the product. The moment you grasp that you are selling Love or Truth, then your Brand becomes much more powerful, because you see it for what it really is – a trick to make others feel safe about who you are and what you are doing. Truth is the most unsafe product there is, and it is the most rewarding product there is. If you are marketing Truth, you have to play this game, or you won't have any real success. Once you have realised that your Brand or product is really an excuse for you to pass a sacred transmission down your fractal line, then you will find yourself an exponent of executive magic. Without really doing anything much at all, your product will market itself, because people cannot resist the Truth.

Making money can be a great deal of fun, if it is done with the sense of detachment that comes from the above truth. You needn't be attached to success or failure, because these two are rarely what they seem. What is essential is your commitment to your Brand, your role within the theatre of your working life.

Prosperity is directly linked to clear commitment – both in our relationships and in our daily work. Within business, there are many cycles that begin and end and begin again. Financial success cannot be measured by a single cycle, but by continued commitment and certainty in one's decision making. Sometimes, when one stays committed to a direction that seems to be unsuccessful, it is often shown to open into opportunities that later become successful. One cannot think one's way through life. One can only align one's inner direction truly, trust in it come what may, and allow nature to do the rest.

The 29th Gene Key

Once you can stand apart from your role and witness your life playing out, you become an exponent of executive magic. The word 'executive' literally means 'to follow out'; so executive magic really means to follow your own magic out into the material world. My personal definition of magic is also very simple – it is the art of doing nothing outside your own nature.

What this means is that magic is everywhere and in everything, and if you simply move from your heart, then magic is the result. This may sound rather trite for the hard-nosed business people out there, but there is nothing soft about making money the easy way. The easy way, as you will see, is through keeping everything as simple as possible. More money is lost to businesses through inefficiency than any other way, and inefficiency is the result of over-complicating life.

SIMPLIFYING BUSINESS AND SELLING YOUR TRUTH

Now that we know that all we are really doing in business is selling our version of Truth, we can have some fun. Contemplating the Gene Key and line of your Brand can be illuminating. Putting this into practise can bring about an instant change in your business - in how you are seen and received by the world at large. People sense honesty at an intuitive level, so when your style of branding matches your inner truth, you come across as authentic and therefore trustworthy. The other element of business that the Pearl brings into sharp focus is the complexity of the business world. We humans have a habit of making decisions that make our lives more complicated. The Pearl invites you to desist from this tendency!

Business is based upon common sense. Good business is furthermore based on basic human integrity. You do not need to get caught up in the great corporate web with its complex, dry and unpoetic language, its obsession with goals and figures, and its general high pressure atmosphere. Business can be exciting, but it need not be stressful.

It only becomes stressful when you feel that you have to step outside your own Brand, and pretend to be something that you are not. When you approach your own business, your creed needs to be about keeping things simple. If you lose touch with the simple, then you will learn a sharp lesson at some point. Staying with your Brand allows you to keep it simple. We have already seen through the Sphere of Culture how the fractal of our allies will reveal itself in time. As long as we balance initiative with patience, good fortune is likely to find us.

THE SHADOW

The Shadow of your Brand will always emerge as a confused message. If you step outside your Brand and try and fit yourself into a suit that does not fit you, then you will create misunderstanding. Your Brand shows you very simply what kind of truth you are here to offer to the world. If you are taken in by corporate conditioning or a lack of self belief, then you will never truly shine in life. You may recall that the Gene Key of your Life's Work, which is the same as your Brand, relates directly to the position of the sun when you were born. This is about how you shine out to the world. Your brightness flows from your naturalness. If you try and force something, you will exhaust yourself. If you hide your light out of fear, you will wither. You are here to shine at something.

The Shadow of your Brand will generally try and undermine you from within your own mind. This Shadow is all about how you see yourself. You have to step into your own shoes and not give into the temptation to try and imitate someone else, no matter how much you may respect them. Look into the Shadow of your Brand and its line, and try and see how these qualities might conspire to undermine you. Once you can see through this Shadow, you will probably experience some kind of breakthrough, as you realise how easy and profitable it really is to be yourself.

THE GIFT

The Gift of discovering your Brand is hugely liberating. Your Brand allows you to be yourself without compromise. The moment you express your truth in the style that feels right for you, you create an immediate buzz. Every human being is a natural salesperson, regardless of their lines. We are all here to sell our slice of truth within the cosmic play. It is all simply a matter of communication. When we discover our Brand, then we feel an instant alignment between our inner life and our outer life. All the love that we have released through the Venus Sequence can pour out through this Sphere. Whatever the style and medium we choose for our self expression, when it comes from our center, it is catalytic and electrifying.

When you look at the central line of Individuation that runs through the heart of your Profile, you can see the power that comes out through your Brand, which is the tip of the iceberg of your Profile. The Gift of your Brand conveys the fruits of your Purpose, it creates a magnetic draw through your attractor field, it is a channel for the pure love of your SQ, and it carries the Gift of the Pearl (which you will learn about soon). When you find the right fit with your Brand, then you will instantly feel at ease inside your bones. Even though you may still face challenges and situations that test you to your limits, the Gift of your Brand will always enable you to centre yourself, and meet the world as yourself.

THE SIDDHI

When you are graced with a vision of your own Siddhis, you may experience them as though they are a single, unified field. Each Siddhi is like an exquisite quality of consciousness, and your Profile is an exquisite cocktail of those qualities. The mystery of the Siddhis is different from person to person. When they do blossom, you may experience a Siddhi that is not even in your Profile. The Siddhis are like that. They do not conform to any set of parameters or rules. Thankfully, there are some things that must always remain a mystery.

What is true however, is that when this light bursts through your being, radiating like a sun from the heart of your DNA, you will always express the quality of the Siddhi of your Brand.

Your Brand is what others will always recognise in you, even though you may not even be aware of it yourself. You will emanate the mystery of this Siddhi. It may be subtle and it may be quite hidden, but if you take the trouble to look at someone you know and contemplate the Siddhi of their Brand, you will soon sense this quality somewhere within their aura. This practise alone can be very powerful, particularly with regards to people who you find challenging! And if you do not wish to trouble someone for their birthtime, you can intuit the Siddhi and line of their Brand. We all carry the potential of this higher consciousness, and it is closer to us even than our own name.

Contemplate the Siddhi of your Brand - dream it into yourself, dive and swoop through its possibilities, and let it be an opening for you into an inner space of great calm and clarity.

THE SIX LINES OF YOUR BRAND

As you contemplate the 6 lines of your Brand, you will see that they each convey both a quality and a method (in parentheses). The quality is what you are here to express through the Gene Key that represents your Brand, so you need to merge both the Gene Key and its line in your mind and heart. You can also do this with the Shadow frequency by imagining what happens when you do not convey this essence, but rather its opposite. The other word - the method - is also very important because it gives you a practical role, and suggests a methodology and language style you can best use to express yourself. This style may well already resonate with your own past experiences and your natural skill set, which should greatly increase your ability to communicate with anyone. Each of the 6 line aspects below are also directly linked to the tone of the human voice. This can give rise to an even deeper contemplation of your Brand.

Line 1 - Boldness (security)

The 1st line always sets the tone of the whole process in each Sphere. In the Sphere of the Brand, all self expression is founded upon boldness. It takes courage to wield one's sword and speak one's truth in the world. We are not here to remain in the background, but to leave our mark on the world in some way. The 1st line is also the line that does its research in the most depth. It has to be grounded in knowledge before it speaks. You will however find 1st lines in all walks of life - whatever they do they will know their subject in depth. This means that others will immediately sense their authority, and feel at ease. You can see that the method for the first line is therefore security. If you are a 1st line, then you are here to put people at ease.

If you were to construct an advertising campaign through each of the 6 lines, then the 1st line would sell its product through the lens of security. They would talk to that part of you that already feels unsafe, and they would couch their product in the kind of language that might allay that sense of fear. Obviously this might sound like manipulation, and this is indeed how the Shadow consciousness bends the mass consciousness to its will. The insurance industry might be an example of the Shadow frequency of the 1st line. This is not a judgement of that sector, rather a metaphorical example of how the 1st line theme can use fear as a means of selling something. At a higher frequency, the 1st line offers people the comfort of its own self-assuredness. If you have a 1st line Brand, then your boldness can put others at ease. The classic archetypal 1st line professions of the world are the emergency services - those experts who arrive in the midst of a crisis and whose calm, self-assured presence immediately puts people at ease.

The above is simply an example of the effect that the 1st line Brand can have on others. The Shadow can unnerve people, the Gift can make them feel safe, and the Siddhi can awaken them.

The 1st line boldness may also be that they are willing to be open, vulnerable, and deeply honest while at the same time remaining strong. This is the kind of strength that inspires a feeling of deep trust in others. When you are contemplating the Gene Key of your Brand, look at it through the lens of the sense of security it can bring others. Look at the Shadow of your Brand, and see the very fear that you are here to help others transform. Whatever your outer work, this is the quality that needs to underpin that work. This is the real outer expression of your Purpose. You are here to help others confront their fears, and inspire them towards self empowerment.

Line 2 - Passion (image)

You may recall that the Sphere of Evolution back in the Activation Sequence also shares the keynote of passion with this Sphere of the Brand. In the case of evolution, the passion is about relationships, whereas here it is simply about the expression of passion through our life and work. As a 2nd line, expression has less to do with content, and more to do with style and performance. This does not in any way mean that the content is any less important - it simply means that the best way for you to communicate is by being creatively free. Sometimes the best way of saying something is by not saying it directly, but through artistic expression, metaphor, or enactment. The 2nd line communicates its essence through rapture, embodied emotion, and movement. Passion has so many doors - as a 2nd line you must find the doors that suit you the best. As a 2nd line you must also trust that the frequency of your message will be understood regardless of how you say it. You are it.

The method for the 2nd line is all about image. This can be about using visual images, either through the creative imagination in a more literal way, or it can be in a more general sense. Passion is demonstrative, unbridled, free. It needs to make an image of itself, a drama, an audio/visual feast. Image is also all about projection. You project a powerful image of yourself, and your message when you have the courage to be utterly free and natural before others. Ironically it is when you forget about your audience, that you are most clearly received and understood. This means however that as a 2nd line, you will have to let go of caring what others think of you. You are here to incite passion through passion, and as long as you stir emotions in a positive way, you are fulfilling your goal. The worst thing is when you leave people cold, or when people are indifferent to your message. If this happens, it is probably because you have not let your imagination run wild enough, and you have not let your heart speak out.

In our advertising metaphor, the 2nd line sells its product using image. It's all about how aesthetic things are, or how beautiful or shocking an image you can leave people with. The 2nd line is here to shake the world up, to provoke, to inspire, and enliven. Take a good look at the Gene Key of your Brand, and imagine how you might project its Gift and Siddhi through some kind of direct or indirect image or metaphor. One of the best ways to sell any product is through beauty. When you create an aesthetic that connects with the higher principles within us, it has a very wide Brand reach. If you can find a way to express your Siddhis aesthetically - through whatever medium you are drawn to, then you are likely to get great recognition and success.

Line 3 - Humour (pleasure)

If you are a 3rd line Brand, then your secret weapon is humour. Having a 3rd line theme as your Life's Work and therefore also your Evolution, means that in life your challenges will always have a 3rd line flavour. This means that you are likely to be the kind of person who packs a lot of experiences into your life, since the 3rd line is all about experiential wisdom. Each of the 6 lines carries its own particular 'built-in' karma, and just by its nature the 3rd line carves its life story out of the unexpected. This is not ever anything to be concerned about - it simply means that you are here to learn from a wide diversity of experiences along the pain/pleasure spectrum. As a 3rd line you may therefore live many lifetimes in your single life, some of which are successful, and some not so successful. From the point of view of wisdom, every experience is a success, because it teaches you to be wiser, and out of this comes your greatest life gift - the humour and perspective that comes from hindsight.

As you contemplate your Brand, look deeply into the Shadow of this Gene Key (and the Gene Key of your Evolution), and see how many stories have emerged in your life through this challenging theme. Your 3rd line may have had issues with commitment in relationships, work, direction. Sometimes you may have attracted people into your life who themselves had issues of commitment with you. Every disappointment in your life is likely there because of this 3rd line theme, but every jubilation is also there because of this 3rd line. All of this continues to enrich your life, and helps you to see the joke of existence. In time this will make you a light-hearted person who can bring solace to others through your compassionate and balanced worldview.

With a 3rd line Brand, you are here to catch the attention of others through making them laugh. Your sense of humour flows naturally from your heart. It is unstudied, warm, sensitive, but also willing to take a risk to make a point. You are a pleasure-giver. Your humour can teach others to laugh at themselves, because you can laugh at yourself. Your humour does not come simply from making light of things as a distraction from feeling the pain of life. Your humour emerges from having felt that pain as deep as anyone. In our advertising metaphor, you sell your product by making people feel good about themselves. When another person laughs aloud, their heart opens, the mind relaxes, and their face softens. You should never underestimate the power of this gift of laughter.

Line 4 - Heart (feelings)

The 4th line is about openness and honesty. It is similar to the 3rd line in that it also engages the realm of human feelings.

Generally you might say that the 1st and 2nd lines have a physical perspective, the 3rd and 4th lines an emotional perspective, and the 5th and 6th a mental perspective. The 4th line Brand is about romance. Romance is a theme that is far wider than its commonly understood meaning. It is about the transmission of a higher ideal of love - a concept that has inspired, elevated, and also confused human beings for millenia. The 4th line style of communication must always be through the Heart, and the human heart is not always at peace. This is not only about pleasure like the 3rd line. This is about the authentic expression of feeling, not just for the sake of it, but within the context of a higher longing.

You might not immediately see the links between prosperity and our modern business world and the above theme of high Romance, but the theme of Heart is everywhere. With a 4th line you are here to put the heart back into business, to remind people that life must have a higher ideal, and we must measure ourselves against that ideal. This does not mean that we have to feel guilty or lacking if our lives take us into difficult waters, rather it reinforces our humanity, and makes us both more humble and more motivated to improve our lot. The 4th line is all about relationships, connections, and bridges, all of which are the key to prosperity on material, emotional, and spiritual levels.

In our metaphor, the 4th line bases its advertising campaign on real human examples. It has no need to conjure an image or make you laugh. It allows others to speak directly out of their hearts, from their pain, and/or their pleasure. And the 4th line will also speak from its own heart, stirring your emotions, sometimes comfortably and sometimes uncomfortably. The power of the 4th line lies in its authenticity and its directness. This is why the 4th line is the most natural salesperson of all the lines - because it engenders trust by telling you how it is, and leaving you to dream of how it could be.

Line 5 - Wisdom (solutions)

As you travel through the epic serpentine odyssey of the 6 lines through your Golden Path, you may feel the various places where the path metaphorically and metaphysically shifts gear. The 5th and 6th lines exist in a different dimension from the 3rd and 4th lines. The 5th line is not focused or even interested in feelings. At its worst it makes use of them to manipulate others, and at its best it uses them to serve others. The 5th line is all practicality, and feelings often get in the way of action. The healthy 5th line also knows that humans are humans, and feelings need to be taken into account. At the same time, the 5th line knows that prosperity is about balance. The 5th line has great inner wisdom when it also learns to listen. Through listening you learn when and how to act appropriately. As a leader archetype, the 5th line can easily act without consideration, but when it acts and considers others, it comes into its greatest power.

If you have a 5th line Brand, then you will have to learn this skill of balancing listening with action. Too much emphasis on either side, and you are out of balance, and immediately you lose your power. As a 5th line Brand, you are here to offer wisdom in the form of practical solutions. If you see someone suffering, you know that the greatest gift you can give them, is to connect them with some form of practical support. This may not come from you, but from someone or something that you have tried yourself, and that you know works. The 5th line also has a flavour of the impersonal to it. This does not make it cold - rather it prefers not to waste time and energy pretending to be something it is not. If you have a 5th line Brand, then your gift is all about practical compassion. This also means that you are a great promoter of the simple and efficient.

In the metaphor of advertising, the 5th line advertisements are all those ones that offer us solutions to the issues in our lives. This is a very different style from the 3rd and 4th line Brand, which engage our feelings.

It is also very different from the 1st and 2nd line Brand, which target our physicality and our sense of security. The 5th line offers you something that you do not have, and it also carries the mystique of hidden wisdom, like a product that has been clinically proven to have a certain effect. You never see those trials, but they carry a great deal of weight. The 5th line radiates this knowledge and wisdom through a profound grasp of its subject. As a 5th line, you must make sure you can deliver what you promise, and when you can, then your message will travel far and fast, and be received with deep and lasting gratitude.

Line 6 - Vision (education)

The 6th line Brand is a visionary. Of all the 6 Brands, these are the people who are most in tune with the long term needs of others. The 1st line can empower people, the 2nd line can mesmerise them, the 3rd line can tickle them, the 4th line can open them up, and the 5th line can guide them. The 6th line has the capacity to completely change a person's worldview.

More than this, the 6th line can change the worldview of a whole community. The 6th line has a vision to convey, and that vision is usually far ahead of its time. There is however no way that this vision can be communicated quickly. The depth of any true vision requires learning, contemplation, and study. This is why the 6th line's only true means of communication is through education.

The 5th line may solve your problems, but there is no guarantee that the problems won't return, and when they do, you will need the 5th line again to help. The 6th line doesn't offer you a solution. It offers you an education, so that the problem can be dealt with at its roots. Then you won't need any solution. You will know how to go within, and find your own wisdom. This is what the greatest teachings and teachers offer - a system that will show you how to find the answers yourself. The 6th line thinks at the 'system' level - it considers how nature works and creates environments in which people can discover for themselves what is best in them and for them. 6th line thinking is relatively new in our modern world. It is new, because it is utterly selfless.

If it is truly successful, then it puts itself out of business! That is the true definition of prosperity - to teach others so well that they no longer need you.

The 6th line however also needs all the other lines to fulfill its great vision. Each line is interdependent in this way. If you have a 6th line Brand, then you are a natural educator. Take a deep look at the Gene Key of your Brand, and consider how you might educate others using that quality. Every Gift is here to inspire and awaken some form of creativity. The 6th line Brand also has to be quite formal and logical in its presentation and communication. In our advertising allegory, the 6th line sells more than just a product - they invite you to come and study the purpose of the product. They invite you to come and learn how to enjoy and understand the product at the deepest level, and they even show you how to make the product yourself. The 6th line always carries this generous transcendent vision that will ultimately lead us all towards a greater collective prosperity.

CONTEMPLATING YOUR BRAND -
LIVING AT YOUR ZENITH

Your Brand is the third Sphere of your Trinity of Prosperity, and as such it represents the transcendent aspect of the first 2 Spheres. The Vocation and the Culture form the base, and the Brand represents their synthesis. In the Brand you reach your zenith, and it is from here that you can receive a vision of your life at its highest. Your Brand is your sword, representing the solar fire that arises from the yang strength of your spine and the yin receptivity of your belly. Your Brand is also your language - the voice and vibration of your soul as it impacts the world. In terms of your embodiment, the Brand is your voice - the expression of your heart through tone and frequency. With a strong vision burning in your breast, your voice carries your fire out onto the winds of fate to stir the forces of change.

Let your life become contemplation in action. The solar energy lifts us up when we let it resonate through our voices. When we speak and sing out our Truth in service to the whole, then we are fulfilling our primary duty on this precious earth. The sun is also nothing but philanthropic. It knows only how to give of itself, which is why it is our greatest role model. In time, the sun will transform all of humanity and the earth into its own image. One day we will become a solar civilisation for our God has always been and will always be the sun. As you go out into the world, let the gentle fire inside your heart sing out on your voice. Speak the words that come from your heart without fear or compromise. Fine tune your Brand to the perfect pitch so that your inner life becomes manifest in your outer life. Let your inner sun brand your name into the lives of those you come across, and leave the world a better place because you are here.

7. THE PATHWAY OF SERVICE

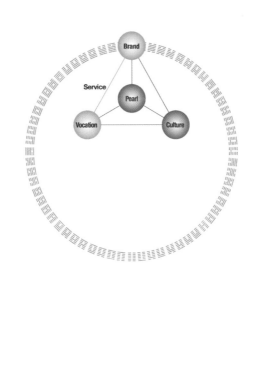

THE PATHWAY OF SERVICE - OPENING THE SOLAR TORUS

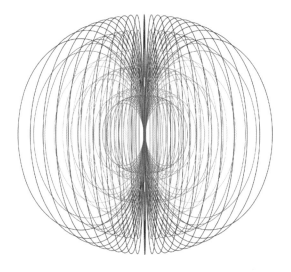

Welcome to the 11th and final Pathway along the Golden Path. The Pathway of Service is very special indeed. It is magical, because it not only completes our Journey, but also opens the way for a quantum leap. The Pearl Sequence represents the mystery of the trinity as a universal, unifying principle. These 3 Pathways of Initiative, Growth, and Service are the foundation of prosperity at every level of the universe. The Pathway of Service also returns our awareness back to the Sphere of our Core once again, although this time we experience a very different flavour emerging from that Sphere. Our wound has become our ally - it has even become our muse. Without this returning Pathway of Service, we would live in a chaotic and dying universe. In the image above you can see the geometric representation of a 'torus' - a dynamic process in which the creative energy within a system is recycled back into the system, giving further fuel and drive to the evolutionary process. This is how all nature works. The tree drops its fruit, which in turn becomes the compost that nourishes its roots.

Scientists still argue about how our sun continues to burn. Where does its supply of fuel come from? There are many theories. One possibility that rings true at a holographic level is that the sun draws its energy from the surrounding space, from the very void into which it radiates its light. To most scientists, this might sound far-fetched, but to the holographic mind it is obvious. Light is born from darkness and vice versa. In order to draw energy from non energy, the sun must also make use of other dimensions. Because it gives of itself unconditionally, it is continually refueled unconditionally. Even though the body of the sun is finite, this principle of balanced energy exchange is infinite. In human terms, it is what makes the difference between wealth and selfishness, and prosperity and selflessness.

The torus is a holistic model of energy dynamics. When we serve the whole, we serve ourself, because we are a part of the whole. The more parts that serve the whole, the more prosperous that whole will be. This is the origin of the Grail question - 'how can I best serve the whole?' As we learn to offer our Vocation and Growth in service to a higher ideal, so our wounds are healed. And like the sun, as we offer ourself in service to the whole, so we receive back from the whole from other dimensions. When you open your heart and give to others, your reward is in the giving itself. Your Pearl Sequence describes this very dynamic at the heart of the torus, which is the central organising principle at the heart of life. All the greatest teachers and teachings of humanity speak to this same truth - that to love and give your best to others is the noblest and highest thing you can do in life.

THE PEARL - A TRIBUTE FROM THE CAUSAL PLANE

The Pearl represents a sacred teaching from a higher evolution. It is rather like an echo from our future travelling back to us to remind us of the great truths. In the Corpus Christi - the mystical seam of the Gene Keys transmission, the human mind is seen not as a mechanical component of our biological brain, but as a subtle dimensional field that our biology inhabits and swims in. This dimension is the mental plane, and our interaction with it takes place through our mental body, our individual resonance with this field. The layer of consciousness beyond the mental plane is known as the Causal plane, and the Pearl is a gift from this plane. The Causal plane begins where logic ends. It opens to us through the doorway of paradox, and once we are through, a whole new world opens up to us.

The Causal plane is the plane of the archetypes - universal symbols that are like the Holographic blueprints of creation. The Gene Keys are such archetypes. They require contemplation to unlock their transmission within us. To travel through the Causal Plane, you must learn the trick of 'synthinking', the ability to think with your heart, mind, and body fully open and receptive. The truths from the causal plane penetrate the heart of our being, and are released from the heart of our being. These truths bend the laws of time and space, and they shatter the delicate framework of logic that many of us covet in order to make us feel safe. To surf the Causal plane you must engage your higher imagination - that faculty of genius that is unlimited by mental constraints and can encompass multiple truths, opinions, and fields without fixing on any single view. The Pearl opens us up to the infinite mind.

TRANSCENDENT THERMODYNAMICS - RE-ENVISIONING OUR UNIVERSE

The following section is a contemplation of various principles that are fundamental to a new understanding of the universe. This is neither science nor philosophy - rather it is a continuation of our journey into the holographic Truth of life. As you read this section, you might like to allow your own imagination to expand to encompass the vastness of a truth that lies outside the capacity of the logical mind. Allow yourself to experience the wonder of 'synthinking' - the combining of heart, mind, and spirit in order to grasp the mystery of a higher Truth.

SYNTROPY AND ENTROPY

The current model of our universe is based on the first and second Laws of Thermodynamics. In a nutshell, the first law states that energy can never be created or destroyed, only recycled. The second law adds to this by observing how all energy flow in our observable universe has a natural tendency to move from order to disorder. This is the meaning of the word 'entropy'. This rather depressing viewpoint of the universe seems to be incomplete. Where is the Gift frequency represented, let alone the Siddhi? There also exists an idea, rather more on the fringe of science, that there is such a thing as syntropy - the universal law that everything in the universe, however chaotic and random it appears, is self-organising, and therefore part of a whole that has consciousness at every level.

Syntropy is the law that underpins the dynamics of the torus - that although life creates greater complexity as it evolves, it is organised by very simple integrated laws. In your life, syntropy can be understood as the hidden higher purpose behind the events of your life. It generates the love in your heart, and the flow of that love is pure syntropy.

Love serves others, and in doing so it serves the whole, and therefore itself. Entropy occurs when the heart and mind meet our own self-limitations, and we are unable or unwilling to move beyond them. When we apply syntropy to our material lives, it emerges as a philanthropic worldview that is selfless and beneficent.

THE FINITE AND THE INFINITE

The problem of science is the problem of infinity. Isn't it a wonderful mystery that our minds are able to even conceive of infinity? The poet Norman Nicholson famously wrote: 'the infinite adjusts itself to our need'. The laws of Thermodynamics are based upon the way energy is seen to behave within a 'closed system'. But Synthinking asks the question: is there such a thing as a 'closed system'?

The scientific mind would like to create a purely objective experiment, but quantum mechanics demonstrates that the human mind may be part of that experiment, so perhaps it can never be truly objective. Our minds are limited by our senses and vice versa. In 2005 I wrote my own Law of Thermodynamics:

Infinite systems exist in infinite dimensions. On account of this truth, the existence of 'closed' systems can be seen as false. The perceived 'openness' of any system is always equivalent to the frequency of consciousness pervading it. It is therefore the degree of 'openness' of a given system to its own multidimensional nature that directly determines the flow of energy through that system.

The finite is simply the shell of the spiritual impulse. The spirit needs the shell of matter to evolve, so it creates and recreates form after form, continually transcending itself. The universe itself is such a shell, so when we are observing the shell, we are really observing something that is relatively finite. It is the animating principle that is infinite. In science, as in so many things, it is so easy to mistake the woods for the trees.

BLACK HOLES AND WHITE HOLES

The black hole is such a beautifully mystical concept. Astrophysicists now believe that at the core of every galaxy there exists a supermassive black hole. This seems to be a deeply holographic Truth. Out of the void emerges the light. The black hole is the representation of the mystical centre of centres. The idea that our universe is omnicentric is both powerful and practical. It is particularly practical when we apply it to our individual lives. Because consciousness is self-organising, it must also be omnicentric. When we awaken the higher purpose within our DNA, then we activate the self-organising principle at the heart of the universe. We attract towards ourselves those forces and allies that allow the whole to reach for a higher harmony. The black hole is the mystery of our Core - the wound that is a gift, out of which emerges our holographic truth and its relationship to the whole.

For every black hole, there must also be a white hole. If all we can see is the black hole, then we will again find ourselves in a universe of entropy - a place ruled by random forces of which we can only be the victim. Below the Causal plane, all the mind can envisage is a world of cause and effect. Beyond the mental plane however, we can see into the causes themselves, and instead of being governed by them, we realise that we are entangled with them. To rise into the Gift frequency or beyond, we must discover the white hole within us. Your white hole is your higher purpose - to awaken from the wound of your separateness, and serve the whole. The white hole is the hidden dimension behind the black hole. Every Shadow contains a Gift, thus only when you pass through the black hole do you find the white hole on the other side. Once you become aware of this higher aspect of your nature, you can increasingly turn towards it, fanning its flames within your life.

TIME AND THE TIMELESS

The black hole holds the mystery of time. Walter Russell, an extraordinary undiscovered genius of the last century famously spoke the words: 'light doesn't travel'. The current mainstream view of the universe is constructed from a so-called empirical view that is based upon the perceived speed of light. Because the speed of light appears to be finite, it also appears that the universe is vast. Our nearest star, the Alpha Centauri system, is 4.3 light years away. In this model, it would take us 4.3 years to get there, if we could travel at the speed of light. This makes us feel like a tiny speck in a vast universe. Walter Russell suggested that light doesn't travel, because it is already everywhere. Light only appears to travel to the human eye, and to the human time-processing brain. The ancient sages spoke of us living within a 'maya' - an illusory world constructed by our brain.

The wave passing across the open ocean doesn't actually move from one side of the ocean to another. It only appears so. The wave is a ripple in the liquid field of the sea. It is the same with light, and therefore time. Time only appears to move. You may wonder if light doesn't travel, then how do we feel the warmth of the sun? We feel it, because we live inside the sun.

Once again, it just appears to us that we live outside the sun. The point is that our means of perception is not as limited as we think. Our current science is founded upon the Cartesian maxim 'I think therefore I am'. Beyond the limited realities of the mental plane our identity begins to merge back into the whole, although beautifully, it does not have to surrender its individuality to do so. A wonderful paradox!

There is a place within you where time stands still. Our spiritual teachers call this, the eternal present. Inside your body at the point behind your navel lies the One Point - the Holographic centre of your universe. As your awareness comes into this point, like a black hole, it swallows time, light, and thought, bringing everything within you into the singularity of being. In the Corpus Christi, this is known as the phase of Absorption, the evolutionary stage that flowers from contemplation. Absorption is the living experience of syntropy, of the white hole within you, of the timeless and infinite present.

GRAVITY AND LEVITY

Gravity is the last great mystery. We of course attribute the idea of gravity to Isaac Newton. Newton's own thinking however continued to evolve throughout his life, and although he became famous for his theories of gravity, he went much further in later life. He was a great explorer of the principles of alchemy. Most scientists see this as an aspect of one man's eccentricity, but alchemy is one of the most misunderstood of disciplines. True alchemy uses scientific method to advance one's own state of consciousness. If we see only gravity, it is once again like seeing only the Shadow. We have unwittingly made ourselves the victim of a forcefield 'out there'. Gravity can be seen as a metaphorical extension of the inner Shadow. We are trapped by the gravity of our thinking.

What if we were to reframe our whole idea of gravity? What if we see it also as levity? The same force that can trap us and hold us down, can also free us and propel us upwards.

Our current notion of transport through space is based upon the science of propulsion. We believe that we must propel ourselves through space to move from A to B. There are other methods of transport. Science fiction has always pointed us towards these higher possibilities and truths. Levity is to gravity what the Siddhi is to the Shadow. Isn't it also interesting that levity also means lightness and laughter? The key is always inside us.

We have to transcend our own thinking, and shift our whole being onto the Causal plane. This requires the opening of our heart to the greater principles of love and service that underpin the entire fabric of our universe.

As our awareness changes to encompass other dimensions and means of perception, so our science may have to start all over again from the beginning. A new science might view the universe very differently. It could not possibly insist of objectivity, which would change the meaning and method of science itself. The future science is about synthesis - to fuse multiple methods, disciplines, and subjects to build a holistic view of the cosmos, where we are no longer the effect of a chain of universal causes. The whole notion of cause and effect is itself a flawed model. With our renewed vision, perhaps we will see another kind of universe that is much closer than we think. This clarification of our awareness has already been described in some detail when we explored the Pathway of Realisation and the Sealing of the Five Senses.

It is always challenging to imagine life before and after a great change. The infinite goes on adjusting itself to our need. We cannot really imagine the consciousness of the people who lived on this earth before the invention of the wheel. Their perception of time and space would have been very, very different from ours. To the people of the future, we will also be seen as a species still existing in a stone age limited by our perception. The Pearl brings us once again back to basics - back to the simple principles and cliches uttered by the wise ones.

To serve the whole is to serve yourself, and there is no power in the universe greater than generosity. These are the kind of insights that come from a contemplation of the 3 Pathways of the Pearl Sequence - Creative Initiative, Sustainable Growth, and Philanthropic Service.

8. THE SPHERE OF THE PEARL

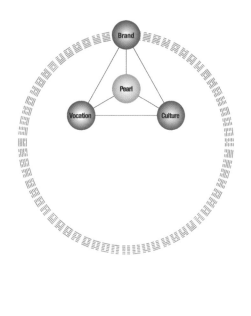

THE SPHERE OF THE PEARL - A QUANTUM WORMHOLE

The final Sphere of the Golden Path gives its name to this third and final sequence - the Pearl. The pearl is an apt symbol for this place of potential inner quietness and harvest. We speak of the 'pearl of great price' or 'pearls of wisdom' to represent something that should be treasured above all else. The Pearl is indeed a precious realisation when it comes to us. It represents that which returns to us from the universe, once we have surrendered to our higher service. It is not quite a reward, for that suggests we may have had an ulterior motive for our service. The Pearl is our harvest. It comes to us only after we have worked at opening our heart, and have offered our love back to the world. The Pearl brings your life into perspective. None of us need as much as our minds believe, in order to be fulfilled. Fulfilment comes through a vision of simplicity.

In the greatest spiritual teachings, there is always a tradition of everything being reduced back down to the essential. In the 10 Bulls of Zen for example, the journey towards enlightenment is depicted in 10 pictures and accompanying poems. The 9th Bull is called 'Reaching the Source'. The 10th Bull however is called 'Return to Society', because the enlightened one now has to once again realise his or her ordinariness. The Pearl is in this sense a wormhole - but unlike most wormholes, it does not lead to another dimension. This wormhole leads us home to our everyday life. It is here, now, in your everyday life where your harvest can be found.

In the Gene Keys, we speak of the 3 frequency bands of human consciousness - the Shadow, the Gift, and the Siddhi. And we speak of the 3 stages of awakening - the art of Contemplation, the phase of Absorption, and the return to Embodiment. Embodiment is not as exciting as it might sound!

There is no Pathway to the Pearl. The Pearl is a crystalisation of all the Pathways that comprise the Golden Path. The Pearl grows inside your being like a child in utero. It is your own private piece of simplicity and truth. The funny thing about the Pearl is that when it arises it brings an end to the complex. It is like a self-destruct mechanism hidden within the Golden Path transmission. Once the teaching is embodied, the teaching is no more.

As we shall see, the Pathway to the Pearl is not a Pathway like the other Pathways of the Golden Path. It is not a Pathway of Contemplation but a Pathway of Absorption. It is the doorway to a new life, a simpler life.

KNOW MAGIC, SHUN MAGIC

There is a mysterious old Taoist axiom that states 'know magic, shun magic'. This is the core of the teaching of the Pearl. The Gene Keys are a wizardly, magical, right brain teaching in a left brain suit. They are a sheep in wolf's clothing. Once you have been afforded the vision of clarity through putting your contemplation into action in the world, you begin to realise how softly and subtly the teachings have guided you back to your true self. Your contemplation continues to take you through the terrain of your life - your purpose, your health, your home, your work, your finances, your friends, loved ones and family, your sexuality, your childhood, birth and conception, and even your ancestral chain right back to the beginning of the universe, and its fundamental structure. The Golden Path knits together all these realms into a single unified field.

Then we have the Gene Keys themselves and your Hologenetic Profile. Despite the seeming complexity of the Gene Keys, they are a fractal wisdom that is infinitely simple. The same truth beats at the heart of every Gene

Key. Your Profile saves your mind a lot of trouble by providing you with a structured journey through the Gene Keys. However, the Pearl invites you to get the joke behind the teachings - behind all teachings - you can pick any Gene Key and any line, and there you will find a truth that resonates with some aspect of your life. This does not discredit your Hologenetic Profile, but it does lend it some perspective. At a certain point when you are ready, you can let go of your Profile, and you can let go of the teachings. This point must come in every quester's life - when the system self-destructs, and you move beyond it into the heart of the magic that is life.

This is the secret meaning of the phrase *know magic, shun magic.*

The Gene Keys are inside you. The Pearl is inside you. The teachings are simply a reminder to keep turning your awareness inwards.

YOUR PEARL - A SIGH OF SIMPLICITY

Your Pearl brings everything down to the essential. In your body, the Pearl brings awareness to your breath. When we discover this awareness rooted in simplicity, then we tend to start sighing. The sigh is a letting go of tension that occurs spontaneously whenever our awareness comes back to our centre. Sighing allows your breath to sink deep into your belly, opening up the diaphragm and energising your spine. That your Pearl brings you back to the fundamental act of breathing says more about it than any words can.

THE SHADOW

The Shadow of your Pearl is about forgetting what is important in life. Because the Pearl is about prosperity, and prosperity is about generosity, this Shadow is about tightness. You become tight when you forget to love yourself.

You get tight when you allow stress to lead you away from the beautiful and the simple. And you become tight when you succumb to the status quo, and compromise a life that could be exquisite for a life of drudgery and monotony. When you contemplate the Shadow Gene Key of your Pearl, think of it in terms of this tightness of spirit. This will be a pattern that prevents you from connecting with others, from relating with nature, and from stepping out into the sun and the fresh air where your breath dances and deepens. The Shadow of your Pearl prevents you from breathing life deeply into your lungs. Every time you sigh, you let go of a piece of this Shadow. It is a Shadow that reminds you how to breathe.

THE GIFT

The Gift of your Pearl is about lucidity. In every one of us there is an awareness that lives behind the events of our life. It is an indescribable kind of clarity. It is neither mental, nor emotional, nor physical, but includes all three. It is not transcendent or lofty, but ordinary and warmth-giving. It is the hearth at the heart of the home. You can use the Gene Key of your Pearl as a contemplative springboard into this lucid inner seeing. Every Gene Key opens a lock, and your Pearl unlocks the mystery of your breath and opens the door to awareness. Awareness is spoken of in so many traditions. It is explored through meditation, and sought through mindfulness. Until you have tasted a single moment of pure awareness you will not have a reference point for what it means or how to further cultivate it. Pure awareness comes in silence, and leaves simplicity in its wake. The Gene Key of your Pearl (and its line) is a path you must follow, and it may take time for you to understand its meaning. Take heart and follow the sighs, and you will sooner or later realise this awareness in your life.

THE SIDDHI

The Siddhi of your Pearl is the place where all words stop. Whatever Siddhi you have in this position, it will silence your mind, and bring you the experience of the timeless dimension beyond thought and thinking. There is nothing further one can say about this.

THE SIX LINES OF THE PEARL

The 6 lines of the Pearl bring an end to the narrative of the lines and Spheres of the Golden Path. These lines describe your version of Prosperity. They also describe your most natural relationship to money, and the true role of money in your life. Apart from bringing us back to a sacred ordinariness, the Pearl can also be about the miraculous. It forms within your life as an organic expression of your own naturalness.

Each of the 6 lines below can release a miracle or series of miracles into your life as a response to your devoted service to the whole. As you contemplate these lines, you might therefore like to open yourself up to the miraculous.

Line 1 - Simplicity

If you have a 1st line Pearl then in your heart of hearts, money really isn't important in your life. We have seen repeatedly how the 1st line is more interested in creation than anything else. Prosperity for the 1st line is about being free to continue to create, so money is needed only to ensure this. This is why the 1st line needs to cultivate a vision of simplicity. You need to learn to live simply in order that you can see clearly, and distinguish the essential from the inessential. If you have a 1st line Pearl, then you are an example and a reminder to others of the value of living a simple life. The worst thing for the 1st line Pearl is clutter. The moment you dispose of your outer clutter, your inner clutter becomes clearer, and the opposite is also the case.

Simplicity is about doing what you love in life. It is about being connected to the source of life, through creativity, through relationships, and through nature. If you have a 1st line Pearl, you must always stay close to nature. Even if you live in the midst of a city, you must find ways to keep this bridge to the natural world alive and thriving. Nature reminds you of the simple purity of life. The foundation of prosperity itself is simplicity. We do not need so much in life to feel free and open and happy. The simpler your life, the happier you will be. Let that be your creed.

Line 2 - Recognition

The 2nd line is a paradox. It loves to display, but it doesn't do it for recognition unless it feels insecure. But the 2nd line cannot help but be recognised for its Gifts, its effortlessness, and its laid-back, natural, and flowing approach to life. This means that the 2nd line is here to learn to receive.

It is so easy for the 2nd line to give and to express its passion, but the way the 2nd line learns to receive is through recognition. When your heart is open, recognition feels good. If you love yourself, then you will always enjoy being recognised.

The Pearl describes the harvest of your life. It is the fruit hanging off the tree that comes after the heart has blossomed in the Venus Sequence. The wonderful thing about fruit is that you can share it with others, and this is what the 2nd line does. It loves to share its fruits and its fortune with those whom it loves. As much as it enjoys recognition, the 2nd line also loves to see others being recognised for their talents (you may recall one of its keynotes is 'the agent'). If you are a 2nd line, you will always enjoy investing in someone you truly believe in.

Your Pearl also describes the effects of synchronicity. It brings surprises into your life as you express your heart and sing out with your Truth. If you are a 2nd line, then prosperity for you is most of all about finding the people in life who you recognise, and who recognise you at a soul level. Look at your Siddhi if you want to know what you are really here to be recognised for. It is out of this quality that money and fortune will inevitably find you.

Line 3 - Celebration

For the 3rd line, there is really only one use for money - it is for celebrating life with others. The 3rd line loves a party. It loves to entertain and be entertained - not in a shallow way, but as an expression of its love of life. Each Pearl represents the crysalisation of a life. What essential principle are you here to embody? In the case of the 3rd line, it is about celebrating life. It is about sucking the marrow out of life, and making the most of the time that we have here. Celebration can be expressed in so many ways - it can be expressed through a life of service and warmth towards others, or it can be expressed through riding an edge that inspires others to their own gifts and greatness. The 3rd line Pearl is a big personality in that they are life's catalysts, rousers, awakeners. The 3rd line will not let you sleep in your mediocrity.

If you have a 3rd line Pearl, it is possible that you will attract a great deal of money into your life. Celebration demands a steady stream of funding! The 3rd line also loves to spend its money on things that increase people's joy. We have to keep remembering that which is essential in life, and one thing that is always essential is enrichment. The 3rd line reminds us that life loves to spend its energy - that a good day ends with a healthy state of exhaustion, because we have used that day to live and breathe deeply. Look at your Pearl if you are a 3rd line, and contemplate the myriad creative ways in which you can celebrate this quality with the world.

Line 4 - Charity

Like the 3rd line, the 4th line loves to share its money with others. However, the 4th line goes about this in a very different way. Charity is a very specific funnelling of the life force for the sake of helping others. Sometimes people are in no state to celebrate, but need practical help because of some misfortune that has befallen them. The 4th line Pearl will end its life having helped many others. Its greatest joy is to touch the hearts and lives of others. You can see how the line structure works - in line 1, life wants only to create, in line 2, its Gifts are recognised by others, in line 3, it celebrates itself, and in line 4, it gives back to the world. Each line plays a role in the harvest of the whole. Because the Gene Keys are a holographic knowledge, we all have aspects of each line, but we also have an emphasis. The 4th line emphasis is always on service.

If you have a 4th line Pearl, then life will tend to bring you together with those in need. When we are able to help others through the use of our Gifts, then we feel great gratitude towards all life. This gratitude is a hallmark of the 4th line. Our love is like a heavy raincloud looking for an arid plain on which to fall. If you are a 4th line, depending on the specific karma of your Gifts, you may also attract large amounts of money in order that you can experience the joy of giving it to those in need.

However, the 4th line is not always about money - it has more to do with service, and there are infinite ways of serving others in life. Contemplate your Pearl, and it will guide you how best to help others.

Line 5 - Power

Line 5 is a line of responsibility. It takes courage in life to assume the mantle of responsibility. Many may come to depend upon you. The 5th line does this as naturally as breathing. The 5th line is here to shape humanity at a much broader level than most of the other lines. Its gift is about wielding power. Power can be held tightly or it can be applied with a soft touch. The 5th line knows that it will always have the greatest impact, when it allows others to be self empowered, which requires the very lightest of touches. With a 5th line Pearl, you are here to bring great positive change into the world. If you have a 5th line Pearl, then you need to expand your vision of yourself to fit such a mission. You are not here to hide your light away, but to stand tall and breathe life into your lungs.

Of all the lines, the 5th line has the potential to draw the most money into their lives. Power requires money on the material plane. In order to serve the whole, that money must be distributed practically and fairly. The 5th line is the modern day Robin Hood - its highest role is to balance the world economy by helping the wealthy to donate their money to those places and communities that are in lack. Unlike the 4th line, the 5th line is not in it for the feeling of reward and connection to others. The 5th line carries out the vision of the 6th line - they are the only ones who know how this can be done. They are the ultimate agents of compassion in action.

Line 6 - Nature

We began this journey through the 6 lines with line 1 of the Life's Work - the Creator. We end with the 6th line of Nature. This 6th line synthesises the 3 phases of Purpose, Love, and Prosperity into one single, simple paradox - that everything is perfect just as it is, and yet still there is so much to be done! The world we humans have created is far from perfect, but it is evolving as we evolve. Our purpose is to open our hearts, and prosper individually and collectively. Nature shows us that there is no such thing as a closed system. Every act is a magical act, and has a direct effect on the whole, and fulfilment only comes through serving the whole.

Each of the 6 lines has its natural relationship to money. The 5th line for example, makes use of it in order to bring about manifestations in the world. The 6th line looks ahead to a time when money is no longer needed. When Christ asked us poetically to consider the lilies in the fields, he alluded to the universal goodwill and balance that exists in the universe. If and when we come to realise our true nature, then money will seem to us the most ludicrous of inventions. Even though it is a symbol of prosperity, we do not need it to prosper if we work together. The 6th harks back to the times of simplicity of the 1st line, but it also knows that we have come a long way from those times. Our future is very uncertain, and if we do need to move through a planetary crisis, it may present us with an opportunity to begin again without money.

The 6th line is both in the world, but not of the world. It knows that we are a part of the great plan of nature, and that nature decides what happens through us. If we create imbalance, then that may well lead to crisis before a new balance is struck. If you have a 6th line Pearl, you are a vision-holder of the truth of sustainability, and at the same time you can be deeply calm and trusting about the direction we are taking. Ultimately, nature is everything. She creates, she destroys, and then she recreates. We are just a pawn in the great game of life.

The 6th line is also in every one of us, and it is embedded within every other line. It holds the keys to the future and the past through an absolute trust of the eternal present.

CONTEMPLATING YOUR PEARL - THE FOUR PRINCIPLES OF MASTERY

The Pearl allows you to put your contemplation of the Golden Path into practise. What use is knowledge if it doesn't step off the page into your life? In life there are wild pearls, and there are farmed pearls. The difference between the two is the same difference between you being given knowledge by another, and you finding it out for yourself. You have to be the pearl diver, and use your imagination to work out how this wisdom can best be put into practise in your life. The Pearl is only for those who are willing to risk their lives for something greater.

Your Pearl Sequence contains four universal principles of mastery and embodiment - they are Strength, Sensitivity, Style, and Simplicity. Everyone is here to excel at something, but few unearth this spirit of genius because of the fears inside us. Mastery is beyond talent, because it excludes effort. It is found in the quantum field of the Pearl. To embody mastery is to realise that the world is your oyster - that is your body, and the pearl is your quintessence. True prosperity is about knowing how to use the time you are given on this earth to do something truly worthwhile. It doesn't matter whether it is grandiose or humble, it must be something worthy of your name.

Mastery occurs when the 3 points of your Pearl Sequence are in perfect harmony - the Vocation, the Culture, and the Brand. When you bring these 3 alive within your life, then the 4th transcendent Sphere of the Pearl brings integration, not only to the Pearl Sequence, but to the entire Golden Path. The 4 principles of the Pearl are therefore a wonderful culmination to this Golden Path journey.

The First Principle - Strength and the Spine

The Sphere of your Vocation is the source of your inner

strength. Inner strength comes from a blend of self-esteem, valour, and vulnerability. Throughout the Golden Path you are invited to be an inner warrior, and to look into the heart of your Shadows. We began with the Pathway of Challenge, and learned how to look difficulty squarely in the face. We then discovered that there was a natural radiance inside us, waiting to break through once we own our own issues. As this radiance is released, so we find the core strength and stability that anchors us in the world. Inner strength is all about the tensegrity of the spine. Your spine very easily holds the tension that keeps you from opening your heart. Once you have released this tension through deep self-acceptance, then you are ready to enter into the mystery of your Venus Sequence.

It takes great courage to look into the genetic wounds that you have brought with you into this world, and yet this is a vital part of your inner strength. Your first invitation in the Venus Sequence was to look beneath the surface drama of your life, and open to the idea that your relationships offer you the greatest possibilities for transformation. There is so much potential for unlocking inner strength, when you are willing to dive into the most vulnerable places, for example your sexuality. We did this when we contemplated the sexual wounding of the Sphere of Attraction. Strength is thus the first principle afforded to you, as you travel this voyage of self illumination along the Golden Path.

The Second Principle - Sensitivity and the Solar Plexus

The Sphere of your Culture symbolises the second principle of Mastery - sensitivity. Sensitivity is a blend of receptivity, empathy, and power. It is powerful, because there is nothing more powerful than unity, and sensitivity allows you to unite your consciousness with your environment. The Golden Path is a calling towards your higher more sensitised nature.

Sensitivity allows you to harmonise with and mutate your environment. A difficult situation or conflict can be instantly dissolved through a sensitive and gracious response.

It is in the Venus Sequence that we really begin to access our sensitivity, as we learn to balance our mind and our emotions - our IQ and our EQ. In the Venus Sequence we learned that intelligence is more than simply an individual phenomenon, but is a connective chemistry generated out of human interaction and relationship. Furthermore, the healing of your deeper wounds allows you to open your heart and experience your original purity and innocence - your SQ. It is intriguing that your heart will only open as you soften your belly, and allow your solar plexus to open first. It is deep in your solar plexus that a future instrument of higher awareness is gestating - this involves the ability to merge your awareness with the awareness of others. Sensitivity is a doorway into this awakening consciousness that is catalysed as we discover our Core Wound, and learn to unlock its higher functioning. The second principle of sensitivity is the perfect counterpart to the first principle of strength. The tensile power of the spine rises out of the softness of the belly like the lotus flower floating in the ecstasy of the mud.

The Third Principle - Style and the Voice

The 3rd principle of Mastery is style. Symbolised by the Sphere of your Brand, Style is all about delivery, and it is a blend of clarity, kindness, and refinement. Your Style is about purity of expression, and requires you overcome the human tendency to imitate others. Style also has a direct relationship to substance, and it needs to complement it and match it, just as one must feel good in the clothes that one wears. Your Style is also about refining your skills and finding an inner 'zone', where everything you say and do expresses the seamless clarity of your perception. Finally,

Style is also about radiating a tone of caring and a genuine intent of goodwill in your work in the world.

In our journey along the Golden Path, true clarity of purpose comes to you when you finally engage the Pearl Sequence. The fruits of that work open a channel inside that clears your perception, and inspires you to begin implementing your higher purpose in the world in a new way. When your heart takes the initiative, and you expand the sphere of your influence, then you grow in prosperity, which in turn means that you have more to give and share with others. Your Style also rides out into the world on the vibrations of your voice. The combination of a soft, open belly and a strong spine meet inside you through your vocal expression, which will carry a new confidence and lucidity. Your words resonate with real power and compassion, and you find that you are heard and recognised at a deeper level than ever before. Your style allows your genius and your gifts to reach others, empowering, warming, and uplifting those whom you touch.

The Fourth Principle - Simplicity and the Breath

The final Principle of Mastery is Simplicity and its embodied principle is the breath. Symbolised by the Sphere of your Pearl, the breath is the great equaliser. When you follow your breath, it will always bring you into your centre. It is a crystallisation of the whole Golden Path, and it reduces everything back to its essence. Every Sphere of the Golden Path is hologenetically folded up within the Sphere of the Pearl. As the clear awareness of the Pearl dawns, so the Pathways and Sequences all fall gently away to reveal this single, simple presence inside all things.

The breath is the principle that brings us into the pause of life. The pause is always there between each in-breath and out-breath. The pause is home to the witnessing field behind all things. It unifies all concepts, it dissolves all boundaries, and it makes all things clear to us.

9. THE PATHWAY OF THE QUANTUM

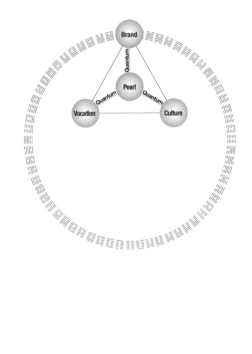

The 12th and final Pathway of the Golden Path comes at the very end. It is an integrative Pathway that brings the whole Golden Path alive at a whole new level. Built into the cycles of life in our universe is a phenomenon known as the quantum leap. Popularised by the science fiction genre, the quantum leap has always been intuited as existing. Some pioneering scientists theorise that it is the only way we could travel to other star systems in our universe – we would have to find a way to break the perceived laws of time and space.

Life does occasionally evolve through quantum leaps. The shift from single-celled life to multicellular life early in our evolution was one such leap. You might say that the evolution of the human brain is also a quantum leap when you compare us to all other creatures on this planet. This doesn't mean to say that we are more intelligent, but it does mean that we have a lot more options than our mammalian forebears. It is not possible to predict a quantum leap in any way, shape, or form. Their nature is rooted in mystery – in the acausal realm. The Pathway of the Quantum suggests that such leaps in consciousness are also built into human biology – they can occur through the synthesis of chemical components in our body, through certain combinations deep within our DNA.

No one can prove that such leaps in consciousness exist. But people have always come into the world manifesting such higher states. In the Pathway of the Quantum, we are entering the realm of the miraculous. Some people say that miracles are simply occurrences not yet understood by science. However, if miracles lie outside the realm of cause and effect, in a hyper-dimensional universe, then they also lie outside the domain of objectivity. The Gene Keys transmission is for the custodians of the great mystery of life. The heart of life is not available to logic, because it defies logic. It is through the Pathway of the Quantum that we witness the truth that the whole is greater than the sum of its parts.

In our biology this is true, because certain chemical and neurological pathways exist that allow our awareness to transcend the sense of separateness that comes with having a body.

The quantum is also true at a collective level – human beings are like individual chemical codes that when arranged and combined in certain formations can give rise to a quantum intelligence – an intelligence so far beyond our individual understanding that we cannot even conceive what it might be like. This is the intelligence referred to in the Gene Keys as the Synarchy. This transcendent possibility and the quantum leap that makes it possible, forms the heart of the Gene Keys transmission. It is captured in microcosm in the 22nd and 55th Gene Keys. We stand on the threshold of such a Great Change. No one knows when it will occur, and in truth no one knows if it will occur, but it seems to be an intuitive knowing held by all human beings. It is not something to hope or pray for – rather it is something just to allow as a possibility, while we continue about our lives. The possibility of the boundless opens the door for miracles.

The Pathway of the Quantum is a Pathway of Absorption. Absorption is the culmination of Contemplation. When contemplation has become an art that imbues your life with awareness and allows you to swim daily in the great mystery, then at a certain stage you will find yourself no longer contemplating. You will forget how to contemplate. You will simply find yourself fully alive. Your life will become ordinary once again. Your seeking will have come to an end, and your Pearl will dawn inside your DNA. This is such a delightful and surprising stage in your evolution. You will become a master of pauses. In fact, the pauses of life become more important to you than the activities that define them.

Your life becomes more musical and more rhythmic. You will smile and laugh more. You will never again forget the essential. Absorption is a stage that you can never fall away from again, because it is already the bedrock of your being.

Above all, you will inhabit the ordinary but remain endlessly open to the miraculous, because your Pearl is a wormhole to the miraculous.

INDIVIDUATION - A CONCLUSION

Congratulations on reaching the end of the Golden Path. You may recall from the introduction to Treading the Golden Path that this wisdom is designed to bring us into a natural state known as *individuation*:

The final goal of the Golden Path is to bring you to a state known as *individuation*. Individuation refers to a process whereby the many different aspects of your life – your dreams, your relationships, your health, your finances, your spirituality – are brought together into an integrated harmony. An individuated human being is a person whose inner life is in exact harmony with their outer life. In such a person, everything has become simplified.

The individuated human being rarely separates him or herself from the marketplace, but is content to move among the world as an ordinary person. Individuation is a powerful and humble place to arrive at in your life. It may not appear exciting to the externally hungry mind, but it conveys the secret weight of the patience and calm that you have anchored deep into your DNA. To be individuated is to court the subtle and the invisible, and at the same time it is to shine out with the light of your humanity.

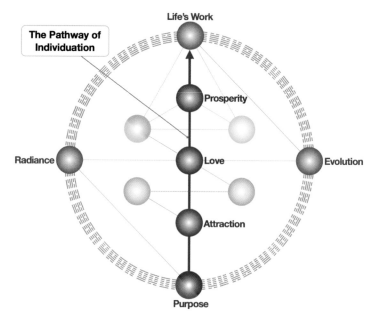

You can see how the central column of your Hologenetic Profile is drawn together via the Line of Individuation. This line only comes about as you complete the Golden Path through the revelation and embodiment of the Pearl. The Line of Individuation integrates the major themes of your life, and is the emergent expression of a higher harmony moving through your being.

THE GENE KEYS TRANSMISSION - INTO THE MYSTIC

At various stages in this Golden Path voyage, I have mentioned or alluded to the Gene Keys as a living transmission of wisdom. In the Tibetan culture, there is a tradition known as the *Terma*. The Terma, which translates as the treasure, refers to a secret spiritual teaching that was concealed in the past in order to be rediscovered and activated much later in the future. The Gene Keys are a terma that has lain dormant for over a thousand years.

They were deliberately hidden within the veils of the Causal plane, that plane of consciousness that lies just beyond the frequency reach of the human mind. They emerged spontaneously within the wisdom mind of a great master in the past, who understood that they would require certain external conditions in order to manifest. Thus the teaching has waited until now to be revealed.

The Tibetans also have a tradition of certain people who are destined to find and unlock the sacred Termas. Such people are known as *Tertons* and *Chodaks* - holders of the lineage of the transmission. Now that you have tasted the Gene Keys transmission, you may find that you can *taste* the transmission behind the Gene Keys at a deep level within your DNA. The transmission is rather like an awakening virus that takes a grip of your inner being, having first established a deep resonance within your own Causal body. If you already have a sense of this, then you are ready to work with the Gene Keys at a deeper level. Having reached the end of the Golden Path, you may now like to consider returning to the beginning and taking in the transmission again with a deeper understanding. Another interesting option is to work backwards through the Golden Path starting here and ending at the beginning.

The Gene Keys in their current form are quite a rarified set of teachings. For many they will simply seem too complex, and therefore perhaps too inaccessible. Because the Golden Path does not require an external teacher, it requires people who are already fairly mature at an emotional, mental, and spiritual level. If you feel called to go deeper into the Gene Keys, then please read on. If you have now had your fill and feel ready for something else, or even for a rest, then I empathise with you and thank you for following it through to the end!

SELF ILLUMINATION

Self Illumination refers to a spiritual breakthrough or a series of breakthroughs that comes about through our own inner contemplation. In the case of the Gene Keys, contemplation is the central technique.

However, contemplation can shift from being just a technique to becoming an art, when we spend enough time learning it. Like any art, it takes practice before the technique becomes a knack, and it takes more practice before the knack becomes an art. When your contemplation does become an art, the process gets far deeper and easier. You may find yourself contemplating a single phrase or word for days or even weeks. Instead of wading through the leaves of words, you allow certain images, ideas, and even memories to become doorways for contemplation.

Self Illumination occurs as we let our contemplation wander freely through our life until it alights on something numinous, something that resonates very deeply inside us. When we discover such an image, word, or archetype then we can spend hours, weeks, and months contemplating it. The simpler the archetype, the deeper it will go inside us until one day it simply detonates, and bang!, we experience Self Illumination, and are flooded by the light within. In the years to come, the Gene Keys may become a popular worldwide wisdom, and if this is so, it will be because those who carry it out into the world will have learned the art of contemplation, and discovered the wonder of Self Illumination. Once you carry the transmission inside, you can further simplify the teachings, and let them emerge from your own Core, through your own Brand, and in your own way. Whatever your level of involvement with the Gene Keys, if you stay long enough with the process and follow the simple guidelines of the Golden Path, you too can experience this beautiful gift of awakening.

THE PEARL IN PRACTICE - AN ADDENDUM

Now you have completed the Pearl and the whole Golden Path, I would like to invite you into an experiment in higher consciousness. If you have enjoyed the Golden Path and would like to be more involved in the Gene Keys teachings or would like to connect up with others following the same path, this section will explain some of the ways you can go deeper and further.

As we have learned through the Pearl, these teachings are about sharing and engendering prosperity and philanthropy. The following model puts the Pearl into practice, so that you can see and experience for yourself a living example of the power of these teachings. In fact if you apply the principles you have learned in the Pearl to your working life and business, then you should find that you will increase your profits and your sense of purpose quite quickly and easily.

THE TRINITY BUSINESS MODEL - SYNARCHY, SYNTHESIS, SYNTROPY

Extending the Synthesis

The Gene Keys are a simple model of a new and sustainable way of doing business. This model is based on 3 interrelated and interdependent pillars. The first pillar is Synthesis. The Gene Keys transmission is based on a vast universal code, and as such it is designed as an interactive open system. This means that if you feel drawn to, you can add your depth and creativity to the growing Synthesis. The Gene Keys model differs from other similar businesses in that it does not operate as a territorial franchise model, nor does it offer formal training or certification. Because the Gene Keys is not about gaining more knowledge, it does not operate as a traditional teacher-based model - rather it is like an omnicentric open university for the soul. The process of Self

Illumination is an interior expansion that cannot be taught, though it can be shared, inspired and supported.

Synthesis thrives on individual human genius, which emerges from freedom. If you feel drawn to working with the Gene Keys, then you are invited to allow your imagination and your intuition to blend with the living transmission, and deepen the Synthesis of this wisdom.

The Gene Keys Ambassador Circle - becoming a lineage-holder

If you are interested in sharing the Gene Keys in any way in the world, you are invited to join our Ambassador Circle, a powerful collective of committed souls who have been drawn to the Gene Keys transmission and are actively sharing it and supporting each other in the process. Becoming an Ambassador is not something to take lightly, as the decision to work with this living wisdom means that you are essentially becoming a lineage holder. Becoming a lineage holder comes with its inner and outer responsibilities. On the inner level it demands that you embody the Truth of the teachings, rather than simply speaking or teaching them. If you are not able to do this, the transmission will tend to give you a sharp lesson in humility. On the outer level, you will also be asked to abide by the core principles of the Ambassador Circle, which involve Honour, Generosity and Integrity. In the Ambassador Circle you can also find out all about our exciting co-creative agreements and other important practical matters such as copyright etc.

If you wish to truly prosper, then you too must embody the spirit of generosity in which these teachings are offered.

Creating Synarchy - hosting the transmission

The 2nd principle of the Trinity Model is Synarchy. Synarchy describes the organic self-organising nature of a like-minded group dedicated to the highest values. Synarchy occurs as those who are extending the Synthesis come together to share, inspire, co-create, and prosper through their ideas and innovations. Over the coming years more and more advanced interactive web platforms will be built that allow synarchies to form.

The Gene Keys Society for the Advancement of Humanity has been established in order that the principle of Synarchy can also form around the sharing of the Gene Keys Synthesis and the Golden Path.

Synarchy is at its most potent when its members move through a transformation together. The Golden Path is designed precisely to support this. To move through the 33 Steps with an intimate group or a loved one is an unforgettable experience. This is therefore something that is strongly recommended and encouraged. Unlike the traditional model where one person who knows teaches those who do not know, the Gene Keys encourages that we *host* the transmission. The host or hostess is a facilitator who acts as the connective hub for a certain group chemistry. Once the group begins, then the host may offer a structure and guide the group with a light touch, but essentially the collective intelligence of the group is honoured. As a host, you provide the alchemical crucible for transmutation, but the change occurs in its own mysterious and unpredictable way. In a sense, all you are doing is providing an arena for the Transmission to work its magic.

The other aspect of Synarchy is its rebelliousness. This is such a wonderful paradox. The Gene Keys awaken individual genius and collective cooperation. Creatively liberated individuals do not naturally tend towards the *herd* consciousness. However, the model of Synarchy demands individual rebellion, not as any kind of Shadow reaction, but as the foundation for higher consciousness. This can also be easily misinterpreted, particularly with regard to relationships and sexuality.

Rebellion is a quality of the spirit, which is not to be confused with social rebellion. You rebel against imitation. You rebel against the tendency of the Shadow to make you believe you are a victim. When therefore a group of such people come together in openness and integrity, the possibility of a higher communion occurs. Then we experience that rarest of things; a harmony of rebels. This is exactly what the Gene Keys Society represents.

Implementing Syntropy

The 3rd pillar of the Trinity business model is Syntropy - that sweet spirit of generosity and higher purpose that underlies every level of the business. The essence of Syntropy is the idea of mutually beneficial exchange. The business must be designed from a 6th line perspective, with the health of the whole in mind.

Today, we can already see 6th line thinking entering the world of business in a more and more pervasive way. This manifests as concern for the environment, the growing importance of Human Resources, and above all a philosophy of sustainability and legacy. Who is the business really for? What is its core purpose and philosophy? Is it philanthropic in the true sense of the word? These are the kinds of questions that come from the 6th line perspective.

Philanthropy is not the privilege of the wealthy, but a requirement of the healthy.

The health of any organism depends on its ability to support and nurture its environment and all those connected to it. The word philanthropy derives from the Greek words *philos* and *anthropos*, which mean love and humanity respectively. As we have learned through the Pearl, generosity triggers a current of goodwill that sends reverberations through multiple dimensions. As you give, so shall you receive.

GENE KEYS GUILDS

The notion of Guilds of Excellence and Learning is an ancient one. In the Gene Keys Society we strive to serve a vision of a better world and the Guilds are a means for us to bring that into physical manifestation. They allow the Synarchy to gather together in groups, either within cultures or across cultures – for the purpose of exploring and extending our understanding of the Gene Keys. Guilds come together in order that we can join our genius and serve a higher ideal. Guilds can be geographical hubs or they can be special interest hubs or both. They can generate new business ideas or they can be purely educational or philanthropic. Their commonality is their very high set of principles and their generous spirit. Each Guild must have a purpose beyond itself.

The Gene Keys Guilds are also hubs of synchronicity. They invite like-minded people to find each other all across the world. They are here to break down boundaries - between people, cultures and points of view. The Guilds invite co-creation around the Synthesis. They involve a sense of adventure, but they also require a real grounding in the laws of our world.

They are guardians of the natural world, and of the principles of fairness and sustainability and philanthropy. In this way, the Guilds unite all three of the principles of the Trinity - Synthesis, Synarchy and Syntropy.

THE GENE KEYS SOCIETY - AN OPEN INVITATION

If you feel inspired and enthused to work with the Gene Keys in any of the ways or contexts described above, please visit the Gene Keys Society website and consider signing up as a member. You will find that the Society is a global hive of creativity and rich interaction, with people working on all kinds of exciting projects and endeavours. Please join your genius to the *genius-pool* and see for yourself the power of the Gene Keys being applied to the real world, tackling real issues, as well as opening hearts and minds wherever they go. We look forward to welcoming you into our ever-growing harmony of rebels!

THE GENE KEYS
GOLDEN PATH
STABILITY

A GUIDE TO YOUR PEARL MERKABAH

A PERSONAL INVITATION FROM RICHARD RUDD

Now that you've completed the Golden Path, and hopefully had a rest, you might be interested in Part 4 of the Path. This is called the Star Pearl, and it is really an expansion to the Golden Path. It takes everything we have learned and applies it into a new matrix that synthesises all the main elements of the Golden Path. The Star Pearl Merkabah is the next step in bringing stability into your life, physically, emotionally, and financially. Your Star Pearl adds 3 more planetary connections through Mercury, Saturn and Uranus, all of which are combined with other elements of your Profile to create a new way of looking at your life as a whole. In the Star Pearl we do away with sequences and move into the actual mirror of our lives. True Stability takes work, and the Star Pearl shows you the specific areas of your life that need to be brought into balance in order for you to experience deep stability and harmony.

Since you have already completed the Golden Path, the Star Pearl offers you a refinement to what comes before, bringing a sense of completion to your process of Individuation. Having achieved this Stability, you are then ready for the higher and more mystical practises of the Gene Keys transmission.

I wish you love and blessings on your continuing journey...

Richard Rudd